For Dan Aaron,
with fond regards
Eric Homberger

THE TROUBLED FACE OF BIOGRAPHY

The Troubled Face of Biography

Edited by

Eric Homberger

Lecturer in American Studies
University of East Anglia

and

John Charmley

Lecturer in English History
University of East Anglia

MACMILLAN
PRESS

First published 1988

Published by
THE MACMILLAN PRESS LTD
Houndmills, Basingstoke, Hampshire RG21 2XS
and London
Companies and representatives
throughout the world

Printed in Hong Kong

British Library Cataloguing in Publication Data
The troubled face of biography.
1. English literature. – 19th century – History and
criticism   2. English literature – 20th century –
History and criticism   3. Biography (as a literary form)
I. Homberger, Eric   II. Charmley, John
820.9'351   PR468.855
ISBN 0-333-41400-4 (hc)
ISBN 0-333-43993-7 (pbk)

Contents

Notes on the Contributors

Lord Blake is Provost of The Queen's College, Oxford, historian of the Conservative Party (1970, rev. edn 1985) and the author of biographies of Bonar Law (1955) and Disraeli (1966). His most recent book is *The Decline of Power 1915–1964* (1985), a volume in the Paladin History of England.

Malcolm Bradbury is a novelist and Professor of American Literature, University of East Anglia. His *The Modern American Novel* and *Rates of Exchange* appeared in 1983, and *Cuts* in 1987.

Hugh Brogan, lecturer in American History, University of Essex, is the author of a study of Tocqueville (1973), and the *Longman History of the United States of America* (1985). His life of Arthur Ransome appeared in 1984. He is currently working on a collection of biographical essays in American political history.

Ruth Dudley Edwards, historian, biographer and novelist, has published lives of Patrick Pearse (1977), James Connolly (1981) and Harold Macmillan (1983). Her biography of Victor Gollancz was published in 1987. She is currently working on a history of *The Economist*.

Victoria Glendinning has written biographies of Elizabeth Bowen (1977), Edith Sitwell (1981; winner of the Duff Cooper Memorial Prize for 1982, and the James Tait Black Memorial Prize) and Vita Sackville-West (1983; winner of a Whitbread Prize). *A Suppressed Cry: Life and Death of a Quaker Daughter* appeared in 1969. Her biography of Rebecca West was published in 1987.

Michael Holroyd has written biographies of Hugh Kingsmill (1964), Lytton Strachey (2 volumes, 1967–8) and Augustus John (2 volumes, 1974–5). He edited, with Robert Skidelsky, the novelist William Gerhardie's posthumous *God's Fifth Column* (1984). He is currently working on the authorised life of Bernard Shaw.

Kenneth O. Morgan, FBA, Fellow of The Queen's College, Oxford, has written biographies of Lloyd George (1974), Keir Hardie (1975; Arts Council Prize, 1976) and, with his wife Jane, Dr Christopher Addison (1980). He published *Labour in Power, 1945–1951*, and edited *The Oxford Illustrated History of Britain* (both in 1984). This volume of biographical essays, *Labour People: Leaders and Lieutenants, Hardie to Kinnock*, was published in 1987.

Andrew Sinclair, historian, biographer and novelist, has written biographies of Warren G. Harding (1971), Dylan Thomas (1975), Jack London (1978) and John Ford (1983). His latest historical inquiry, *The Red and the Blue*, a study of 'Intelligence, Treason and the Universities', appeared in 1986.

Robert Skidelsky, Professor of International Studies, University of Warwick, has published *Politicians and the Slump* (1967), a study of English progressive schools (1969) and a biography of Oswald Mosley (1975). The first volume of his life of John Maynard Keynes, *Hope Betrayed 1883–1920*, appeared in 1983.

Hilary Spurling has written a handbook to Anthony Powell's *A Dance to the Music of Time* (1977). Her biography of Ivy Compton-Burnett appeared in two volumes in 1974 (*Ivy When Young*) and 1984 (*Secrets of a Woman's Heart*), which won the Duff Cooper Memorial Prize for 1984, and was joint winner of the Heinemann Award. She is currently writing a life of the novelist Paul Scott.

Ann Thwaite has written lives of Frances Hodgson Burnett (1974) and Edmund Gosse (1984; winner of the Duff Cooper Memorial Prize for 1985). She is currently writing a biography of A. A. Milne.

Introduction

In an age of academic specialisation, biography is a curious anomaly. Its appeal crosses traditional fields and forbidding disciplines; the life of an Einstein, a J. Robert Oppenheimer or an Alan Turing rightly commands a broad public interest while the technical achievements of such men remain forever a closed book to most readers. The people who write biographies are generally outside academia, and reflect less the institutional concerns of a discipline than a range of more traditional and sometimes personal motives: wanting to tell an interesting story, to resurrect a wronged or neglected reputation, to reinterpret the role of an individual. The British above all others pride themselves on the glories of their biographical literature. But, and there really is no contradiction, these same British have been the least concerned to study biography with anything like the attention which they have brought to other forms of writing. Biographies are widely read; they make up an important proportion of books published in the humanities; but they are for the most part unstudied, unexamined. The spirit which prevails in British biography is commonsensical, empirical and humane. We do not suppose that better biographies will necessarily result from closer attention to the assumptions and practices of the craft: but different biographies may be written, ones which are a little less redolent of the biographical clichés and formulae which too often seal off another consciousness from ourselves.

We learn from biography, it brings us closer to the reality of other people's lives. Inevitably, perhaps, certain biographies become as much meaningful events in a 'life history' as the novels and poems one has read, the plays seen, even the acquaintances one has met. The broad appeal of biography is reassuring. It suggests that in our interest in the lives of others there is at least the possibility, the hint of a surviving common culture. But everywhere in academic life the subtle, the not-so-subtle denigration of biography grows apace. In the social sciences, social history and in the high reaches of critical theory in the study of literature, influential voices tell us that the 'author' is dead, and that biographical study of a writer or artist is either irrelevant or not fully serious. Roland Barthes argued in an influential article in 1968, 'La Mort de l'Auteur', that

The image of literature to be found in ordinary culture is tyrannically centred on the author, his person, his life, his tastes, his passions, while criticism still consists for the most part in saying that Baudelaire's work is the failure of Baudelaire the man, Van Gogh's his madness, Tchaikovsky's his vice. The *explanation* of a work is always sought in the man or woman who produced it, as if it were always in the end, through the more or less transparent allegory of fiction, the voice of a single person, the *author* 'confiding' in us.

Criticism after the publication of Barthes's article can never return to a state of primal innocence, not least because for half a century or more there has been no such simplistic belief among those who sought to raise criticism to full seriousness about 'confiding' authors. No historical biographer would be guilty of such naïvety. Is the literary culture which produced 'How Many Children Had Lady MacBeth?' in some profound way mistaken about the proper relationship between literature and life? But the way Barthes holds the *'author'* before us has proven remarkably seductive. What may have been in 1968 a polemical overstatement is now entrenched academic dogma. Ironically, few critics have written as brilliantly as Barthes about biography as a form of literary discourse (see his essay in *New Critical Essays*, trans. 1980, on Chateaubriand's life of Rancé), or have been as deeply engaged in the interpretation of the 'common culture'. But, as Robert Skidelsky argues, the biographical programme is deeply troubled.

In view of the uncertain position which biography occupies in academic life, the School of English and American Studies of the University of East Anglia agreed to fund a conference in 1985 at which practitioners of biography would be invited to reflect upon their own practice, and upon the state of biography today. The present volume is written by participants at the conference. Three contributors, for varying professional reasons and other commitments, were unable to write something for publication, but Ann Thwaite, with whom the project was discussed at an early stage but who was in Japan when it was finally held, agreed to write as though she had been present. The contents of this book are not the proceedings of a conference, but the further reflections of those who took part in the discussions. We feel it stands on its own as a contribution to the current debate over the place of biography in our culture.

In one of the Czech writer Milan Kundera's stories in *The Book of Laughter and Forgetting* (published 1980 in translation) there is a speculative passage about biography:

> Every man has two erotic biographies. Usually people talk only about the first: the list of affairs and of one-night stands.
> The other biography is sometimes more interesting: the parade of women we wanted to have, the women who got away. It is a mournful history of opportunities wasted.

For every 'official' biography, and even for those written wholly without official blessing, there is a shadow or phantom story, 'the other biography', forever unwritten, but of which biographers endlessly scheme to catch a furtive glimpse. Biography is a massive socially sanctioned invasion of the privacy of private life; we have become the most voyeuristic culture in history. As Paul Roazen put it in *Freud and his Followers* (1975) 'it is impossible to establish a man in history without compromising his privacy'. Biography seeks to do what only the greatest art has ever done: to convey the feel of an individual's experience, to see the world as a single person saw it. Because it aspires to the incommunicable and the inexpressible, it is no wonder that biography is provisional. There can never be a definitive biography, merely a version, an attempt, an essay which in time reveals how completely all such attempts bear the impress of the age in which it was written. Few biographies last. Not only do certain subjects seem, over time, to be more or less interesting, but the frame of interpretation, the cultural luggage, can change so comprehensively that the important biographies of one age are the library discards of the next. Ours is a century distrustful of exemplary lives in the heroic sense: we must have T. E. Lawrence raped and tormented, and F. Scott Fitzgerald asking Hemingway to have a look and tell him if his penis was adequate for manly duties with Zelda. Such moments in biography bear the unmistakable brand of our culture. And how quickly one senses the possibility that concerns like this may seem derisory to a later age. (It is nice to note, however, that feminist biography consists largely in the presentation of 'role models' among 'our foremothers, our sisters, our heroines' as a critic, Elizabeth Kamarck Minnich, observed in the Summer 1985 issue of *Feminist Studies*. Biographies of women by women, such as Young-Bruehl's Hannah Arendt (1982) 'bring back to us . . . women we can now admire as friends'. [Young-Bruehl may not exactly welcome this sort of sisterly attention.] Who said that Victorian biography could never make a comeback?)

Even in an age of surfeit, of a choking overabundance of information, the lives (and consciousness) of most people remain unwritten. Biography as we have it has scarcely begun to deal with ordinary life. Even in the age of mature democratic societies, the biographical tools and also the moral commitment do not exist to deal with the invisible ones. The lives of those whose activities were recorded in the press, whose contemporaries saved letters, who wrote books or who made an impact upon affairs, upon opinion, upon the shape of their age, have traditionally been the terrain of biography. Different tools might be required to write about the lives of those others, who shared experiences common to most ordinary people: housing conditions, the family, religious affiliation, education, politics, employment, children. The life of an ordinary person contains within itself a meaningful range of the social history of a society. Recent work in anthropology (Langness and Frank, *Lives: An Anthropological Approach to Biography*, 1981) and psychology (Runyan, *Life Histories and Psychobiography*, 1982) suggests that the procedures of the biographer are increasingly of interest to the social sciences, while they are under direct attack in the humanities. Perhaps the significant advances now will come from the anthropologists, whose preferred term is 'ethnography', who have shown how uncertain the Western concept of 'a life' is for describing non-Western peoples. They have made us aware that our conception of biography is culturally determined, an ethnocentric assumption.

The division between literary and historical biography, which Leon Edel noted in his Alexander lectures in 1957, does not quite take on the same form it did two decades ago. The differences between the historical and the literary forms of biography are well illustrated by the contributions made by Lord Blake and Victoria Glendinning to this volume. All forms of biography have become increasingly frank about sexual activity. This is no longer a direct part of the legacy of Freud's contribution to biography, his psychoanalytic study of Leonardo da Vinci (1910), but a reflection of a more pervasive and diffused recognition that sex and gender are not the background of an individual's life, not the interludes, but are part of the foreground as well. The Victorians, who generally knew about such things but did not believe it was acceptable to talk or write about them, simply drew the line in a different place than we do. In his *An Autobiographical Study* (1935), Freud remarked that

The public has no claim to learn any more of my personal affairs
... I have ... been more open and frank in some of my writings
... than people usually are who describe their lives for their
contemporaries or for posterity. I have had small thanks for it, and
from my experience I cannot recommend anyone to follow my
example.

The sexual practices of W. H. Auden and Joe Orton do not quite
shock contemporary readers of their biographies, as those of
Swinburne and Wilde would have horrified their contemporaries;
and to learn that 'for Christopher, Berlin meant boys' when
Isherwood rewrote *Goodbye to Berlin* (1939) in *Christopher and his Kind*
(1976) is simply a sign that we live in a more tolerant climate. The
sexual dimension of Bourne's *Palmerston* (1982) fundamentally
alters our perception of how Palmerston operated, and restores to
us a part of his character appreciated by contemporaries but ignored
by Victorian hagiographers. We learn that the Queen did not like
Palmerston, but gentlemanly Victorian biographers struggled to
convey the reasons why; once it is appreciated that he was the sort of
libertine who tried to seduce one of the Queen's ladies-in-waiting at
Balmoral, this becomes more explicable. It is hard to envisage a
future in which Victorian reticence will replace our sexual frankness
in biography; our 'lies and silences' are on different subjects.

Biographers share with novelists (and autobiographers) a love
affair with narrative. The oft-noted comparison of biography to the
Victorian triple-decker, with its vast range of characters, detailed
social observation, and rich sense of place, has been interestingly
restated by Cynthia Ozick:

A good biography is itself a kind of novel. Like the classic novel, a
biography believes in the notion of 'a life'—a life as a triumphal or
tragic story with a shape, a story that begins at birth, moves on to a
middle part, and ends with the death of the protagonist.
(*Art & Ardour*, 1983)

Traditional novels, too, have a commitment to 'a life'. The novel and
biography long cohabited within similar narrative structures, from
Defoe to *David Copperfield*, but the foregrounded story, the authorial
presence, traditional chronological design, and the stately scene
setting of the major biography are no longer typical of contemporary
fiction. Consider the following:

The morning of October 15, 18—, was drizzly, and the East River heaved dull and gray as R——'s ferry pushed out from Brooklyn. On Bedloe's Island, far across the Bay, he could mistily make out the silhouette that had been tantalizing New Yorkers for months; an enormous, headless Grecian torso, with half an arm reaching heavenward. But he probably gave it no more than a glance. His mind was on politics, and on this evening's Republican County Convention in the Grand Opera House. He was curious to see who would be nominated for Mayor of New York.

This could easily be a misplaced pasage from William Dean Howells, or a host of other novelists in the realist persuasion, except that a novelist need not bother with the careful speculation about whether the subject did or did not think about the incomplete Statue of Liberty; the novelist would know, the biographer in all likelihood cannot. In every other respect the passage, with its careful scene setting, and delayed presentation of the subject's central concerns, suggests how comfortably the contemporary biographer works within the narrative structures of traditional fiction. Within two pages we are told that soon after disembarking from the ferry he learned that he was to be the Republican nominee for Mayor of New York in 1886. The author, Edmund Morris, has many such literary graces and flourishes of speculation in his magisterial *The Rise of Theodore Roosevelt* (1979). But he is not watching himself watch the young Roosevelt (that may be part of the way he writes President Reagan's biography); he is not pointing out that 'a person of curiosity' could have deduced several strong possibilities about a couple walking on the quay at Lyme Regis 'one incisively sharp and blustery morning in the late March of 1867', as John Fowles does in the beginning of *The French Lieutenant's Woman* (1969). The self-reflexivity, ontological uncertainty, distrust of the structures of explanation, the uncertainty over 'the real' and 'the fictional' have not yet transformed the story of the young Roosevelt into a literary invention of Edmund Morris's. American biographers, no less than their British counterparts, seem comfortable with the novelising of their subject's experiences: how Thomas Hardy would have enjoyed the opening paragraph of the first volume of Alan Bullock's life of Ernest Bevin:

The ancient forest of Exmoor lies in the extreme west of Somerset. Bounded on the north by the Bristol Channel, it is separated from the Brendon Hills to the east by the valley of the River Exe. In the second half of the nineteenth century it was still an undisturbed, remote part of the West Country. . . . The traveller coming from the east might follow the high road up the wooded and winding valley of the Exe as far as Exton, but there the high road bore off north towards Dunster and the coast, leaving him to cross the bridge and push on up the Exe to Winsford, a village of not more than five hundred souls under the eastern edge of the moor. The surrounding hills and the close-set woods along the river valley combined to shut Winsford off from the outer world; its only link was the carrier from Dulverton calling once a week.

It was here that Ernest Bevin was born on 7th March 1881.

Even Bullock's title, *The Life and Times of Ernest Bevin*, vol. 1: *Trade Union Leader* (1960), invokes the memory of Victorian novels.

If all biographies were subtitled 'A Story', and if biographers set out as consciously and gravely as Bevin's biographer to use the devices of the novelist to adorn their efforts, the *literary* nature of their concerns would be even more visible.

It may be a matter of time before biography, loosened from its roots in fact and document and 'truth', and bolstered by the techniques of fiction, makes its appearance. Will such books be biographies in the traditional sense? Those who regard biography as an instrument of historical understanding will continue largely as they have ever done. But for others, perhaps more attentive to the troubled face of biography in our culture, the uncertainties deepen. The suspicion of traditional biography is so intense in the social sciences, history and in the vexatious kingdom of high literary theory that wild heresies, tremendous flights of the persecuted biographical imagination, loom on the horizon; Hugh Brogan's comment that unless a biographer 'feels a strong commitment to the truth of his subject, he ought not to touch it' seems to us a deeply controversial and necessary assertion for the future of biography.

School of English and American Studies   E.H.
University of East Anglia, Norwich   J.C.

1

Only Connect: Biography and Truth

Robert Skidelsky

Biography is going through one of its bouts of being boosted as a serious activity. It is one of the 'major literary genres of the twentieth century' according to Jeffrey Meyers. Yet there's something inescapably second-rate that seems to cling to biography and its practitioners: 'gossip-writers and voyeurs calling themselves scholars' was how W. H. Auden described them. Certainly their scholarly reputation has never matched their sales. Scholars are far from convinced that biography has any important light to throw on art or history. And by the general public biographies are read chiefly for their gossip.*

There is a curiosity in all this, for undoubtedly contemporary biography is more scholarly and takes itself more seriously than ever before. Biography in Britain used to be a mixture of hobby and hackwork. Anyone it was felt could do biography who put half a mind to it. Indeed, half a mind was usually all the subject got, since biography, as a well-known retirement pastime, was frequently a matter of the half-dead chasing the dead. Or it might be done by journalists in their spare time. There were also 'professional' biographers, sad and untalented people one thinks of them, hopping unmemorably from one 'life' to another. True enough, distinguished writers and scholars dabbled in biography. But they were not distinguished *because* they did so; and indeed their distinction was a little tarnished by their excursions into the genre.

---

*This may be illustrated by an incident which took place at the conference which gave rise to this book. Michael Holroyd, Susan Crosland, Hilary Spurling and myself were sitting in a student kitchen late on the opening night, drinking some tepid liquid concocted from various tea, coffee, milk and sugar-type substances supplied by the organisers, when we were joined by members of another conference, who had apparently spent the evening discussing problems connected with the disposal of industrial effluent. 'And what do you do?', one of them asked us. 'We are biographers'. 'Oh, you write about sex' came the immediate and confident reply.

To a great extent all this has changed. Today's biographer is likely to be a professional scholar, an expert in his subject's time, place, and activity. He is likely to come to the biographical task with all the apparatus of modern scholarship: original sources, a critical attitude to evidence, precise referencing and so on. Moreover, whereas the old-style biographer thought of his work chiefly as a memorial (often he was an old family friend), the modern biographer is equipped with sophisticated biographical credos: one can scarcely open a contemporary biography without reading, usually in the preface, a justification both for doing that particular biography and for biography in general. There is even an 'interdisciplinary quarterly', *Biography*, published in Hawaii. Yet in this very reiteration of biography's claims there is more than a trace of unease: a feeling that it has not yet fully won its intellectual spurs. And this feeling is justified. Biography is still not taken entirely seriously as literature, as history, or as a cogent intellectual enterprise.

The problem is two-fold. The first part has to do with the weakness, or difficulty, of biography's central justification, namely that knowledge of the subject explains or illuminates his or her achievements. Biography had its roots in the Romantic view of the artist as Hero and in the Great Man theory of history. Here it is only necessary to point out that the kind of claim to understanding of achievement – in terms of the personality of the achiever – implied by such conceptions is now rejected by many scholars. 'Biographies of writers', Auden wrote, 'are always superfluous and usually in bad taste.' No knowledge of the raw ingredients, Auden continued, 'will explain the peculiar flavour of the verbal dishes he [the writer] invites the public to taste: his private life is, or should be, of no concern to anybody except himself, his family and his friends'.[1] Contemporary fashion in literary criticism has gone even further. Not only is the personality of the author irrelevant to understanding the text, it is now the reader who is supposed to 'deconstruct' its meaning for himself. There has been a parallel, though not identical development, in historical studies. Most historians now reject the Great Man theory of history – the view that historical events are caused by, or bear the imprint of, or would have been very different but for, the unique personalities of leading actors. The most common view is that the hour produces the man – not the other way round. Even if the biographical approach can explain or illuminate achievement, it may not explain or illuminate much. Authorial idiosyncrasy may be a quite minor factor in the genesis of a literary or historical event, or in the shape it takes. To treat it as a major, or the major, factor is to distort our understanding of the event or trivialise the achievement: to rob it of its public and universal attributes.

The second part of the problem has to do with the way biography is in fact done. Even if knowledge of the life can, in principle, deepen our understanding of the work, a great deal of that which biography conveys, and is required by modern convention to convey, may be irrelevant to that particular task. To this charge the biographer may reply that better understanding of his subject's life, not his work, is what he aims at; the latter, if it is achieved, is a bonus or by-product. But this defence (or retreat) is not without difficulty. Why write about Napoleon or T. S. Eliot rather than about Mr Smith or Mrs Jones? Surely it is because of what they have achieved. We are curious to know more about such people *because* they have done extraordinary things; we expect that their biographies will help explain how they came to do these things, and illuminate the achievements for which they are remembered. It is then rather lame for the biographer to respond that he is in the business of telling a story about people who happened to be called Napoleon or T. S. Eliot; that their lives are full of human interest; and that he 'hopes' that his story will 'shed light' on the question of why we want to read about them. We may feel that this reply is a biographical evasion; that not all people are worthy of having lives written about them; that the task of illuminating the human condition in general is better handled by fiction than by biography; and that if biography cannot in fact tell us something important about Napoleon's historical or T. S. Eliot's poetic achievements it is not *serious*; which is not to say it may not be entertaining, revealing, pleasure-giving, popular and so on.

The two problems with modern biography – the difficulty of its central scholarly justification and the way it is done – are connected, though the first would exist however biography was done. That is to say, the current cult of biographical 'frankness' often seems to be a distraction from the task of connecting up the life and the work. Although it is often justified as a contribution to that end, it has become an end in itself, part of the current obsession with the private lives of the famous, dignified by a high-sounding pro- gramme of 'truth-telling' in much the same way as journalists defend tittle-tattle about the Royal Family in the name of the public interest'. Nobody is (or ought to be) against truth. What I want to suggest is that biographical 'truth-telling' today has come to mean something which was no part, or only a small part, of its original truth-telling programme which developed after the First World War.

Two truth-telling impulses fed the attack on the Victorian model of biography. The first was the rejection of dishonesty about the subject's private life. The second was rejection of the Victorian scale of values - the judgements which Victorians put on lives and achievements. Both were attacked in the name of 'truth'. The first is very obvious; the second is more subtle. Essentially the charge was that Victorians honoured the wrong things, worshipped false gods. If the first impulse aimed at honesty in description, then the second aimed at 'true' moral judgement. Although Lytton Strachey, the father of modern biography, has been generally identified with the first position, he is much closer to the second. We need to distinguish between the two breaks with the Victorian tradition to understand what has happened to the post-Victorian biographical programme.

A standard view of 'what was wrong' with Victorian biography (and why) was put by Lord Birkenhead in a letter to Felix Frankfurter, dated 14 March 1962:

> This appalling practice [of hagiography] played havoc with mid-Victorian biography. . . . The only hope . . . is to seek for the truth, however awkward it may prove for one's subject. . . . The biographer must be able to stand . . . outside his subject and survey him with icy objectivity. . . . The trouble is that when one is writing a book at the request of a widow or a daughter, it is sometimes very difficult to get this point into their heads. They see the adored one in a far rosier light, and are inclined to be pained by the surgeon's probe.[2]

The critique of Victorian biography was that it covered up unpalatable facts about the subject's private life, usually at the behest of the family; the suggestion was that it was the contractual relationship between the biographer and the 'widow' which kept biography dishonest.

It is obvious, though, that what Victorian biography was and was not allowed to say depended as much on the reader as on the widow. In his life of Leslie Stephen (1984), Noel Annan notes that both Stephen and his friend James Russell Lowell shied from indecency in literature and judged that a biographer betrayed his trust if he unveiled any weakness which should have been left in modest obscurity. Great was Lowell's rage when Froude asserted that Carlyle was impotent and the great prophet's marital life was a model of incompatibility. Stephen said he was equally shocked; to publish such stuff now was 'a needless outrage'. Lowell deplored the fact that 'biography, and especially that of men of letters, tends more and more towards these indecent exposures. . . . There are certain memoirs, after reading which one blushes as if [one] had not only been peeping through a key-hole but had been caught in the act'.[3]

Victorian biography reflected Victorian sensibility. Certain things were not talked about in decent society. Just as importantly, biography was regarded as exemplary. The Victorian age was one of hero-worship. In a period of religious doubts, morals increasingly needed the support of exemplary lives: lives which, in particular, stressed the strong connection between private virtue and public achievement. That the leading apostle of hero-worship should have been revealed as sexually impotent was a thought too uncomfortable for the Victorian mind to entertain: hence the outrage of Froude's revelations. Froude's life of Carlyle (4 volumes, 1892–4) is now considered one of the few adornments of Victorian biography – an essay in truth-telling made possible by Carlyle's remorse at the way he had treated his wife, and by an admiration on the part of Froude for Carlyle so total that, in Lytton Strachey's words, 'it shrank with horror from the notion of omitting a single wart from the portrait'.[4]

The reasons for the elements of deception in Victorian biography are thus complicated. Lives were cleaned up not just because readers 'shrank from indecency' (though this was certainly important) but because they were expected to exemplify virtues, private and public. It is often forgotten that public lives were whitewashed just as much as private ones: public men always acted from the highest motives. Finally, the Victorian way of doing biography reflected a widespread agreement as to what the virtues and vices actually were – that is to say, there was an agreed standard for judging character and achievement; and a common (though highly superficial) view of their interconnections.

This complex of understandings and agreements was shattered by the First World War. The modern biographical movement was shaped by the experience of that war, and the loss of faith in leaders and in the official values which it caused. Modern biography - the movement we date from Lytton Strachey's *Eminent Victorians* (1918) – was above all debunking biography. Its purpose was to expose eminent characters as humbugs or prisoners of false values. Truth-telling for the modern biographer was not simply fidelity to the facts or scrupulous reliance on 'original sources': it was to do with correct moral evaluation. And no moral evaluation was considered correct which esteemed characters and attitudes and policies which had contributed to the mass slaughter.

It is worth taking a closer look at Strachey's aims and achievement. He wanted to make biography a work of art, marked by brevity, selection and design. What particularly rankled with him was the fact that 'the most delicate and humane of all the branches of the art of writing has been relegated to the journeymen of letters'. But he also insisted that a biographer must retain absolute freedom of judgement: 'It is not his business to be complimentary; it is his business to lay bare the facts of the case as he understands them.' Strachey made it clear that he was not in the business of exhaustive truth-telling: 'I have sought', he wrote, 'to examine and elucidate certain fragments of the truth which took my fancy and lay to my hand.'[5]

Biography as art and biography as truth were very much bound up together in Strachey's mind. First of all he was trying to escape from the Victorian idea of the biographer as family retainer, whose job it was to ensure that nothing went wrong with the literary funeral arrangements. The traditional biographer's job was to embalm his subject in the greatest quantity of his own prose that it was thought that readers or publisher would tolerate, with such linking commentary as to exhibit his character, motives and affections in the noblest light. In arguing for an improved quality of biographer Strachey was staking the claim of biography to independent judgement. But it was just as important for Strachey that the form of biography should express the moral viewpoint of the biographer. For Strachey this was primarily aesthetic. He judged his characters from the standpoint of the man of letters. Strachey is one of the few modern literary figures who has written about men and women of action. He brought the values of the artist to bear on the actions of the doers. This is a part of his truth-telling programme which has been largely scrapped. Literary and historical/political biographies have become two separate genres, with their own writers and their own conventions. Biographers have on the whole ceased to be family butlers in the narrow sense, but have remained butlers in the wider sense noticed by William Gerhardie of 'echoing' the values of the class of persons they write about, because they themselves are attached to it: literary persons write about literary figures; historians and political scientists write about historical actors and politicians.[6] The gain in scholarship is purchased at the cost of independent judgement, in Strachey's sense.

One final point needs to be made about Strachey. His standard of value was not just that of the man of letters: indeed, it would be impossible to claim that any unique, certainly any uniquely pacifist, pacific, or humanitarian outlook is entailed by such a background. He judged his characters in the light of G. E. Moore's ethics, convinced, as was Keynes, that Moore had discovered 'the rudiments of a *true* theory of ethic'.[7] Moore took over Plato's idea that the highest good is always that which is desirable in itself and not for the sake of anything else; took his final good, therefore, to be an attribute of states of mind rather than states of action; and characterised the best states of mind as those attuned to 'the pleasures of human intercourse and the enjoyment of beautiful objects'. This provided Strachey with his ethical standard for judging 'lives', deployed most clearly in *Eminent Victorians*. The essay on Cardinal Manning in particular is a dramatisation of the conflict between doing good and being good, between the Aristotelian 'good as a means' and the Platonic 'good as an end'; and Strachey's sympathy is overwhelmingly with Cardinal Newman. The point to emphasise is that 'telling the truth' for Strachey did not entail what Leslie Stephen would have called 'prying'. What it did entail was not taking the characters and achievements of his *Eminent Victorians* at their conventional valuation. The do-gooders turn out to have bad characters; their good works monuments to misplaced energy. Strachey's methods were, in fact, amazingly pre-Freudian. His *Eminent Victorians* were certainly driven by demons, but sexual repression is barely hinted at, and he has no model of the economy of the psyche, with its balance of drives and sublimations. Essentially his truth consisted in not calling something bad good. Strachey wrote morality plays with the morals turned upside down.

Such assurance in the matter of ethical judgement could not survive the eclipse of all 'objective' theories of ethics; or the subsequent course of history. The biographical revulsion against men of action – the warriors and statesmen, abetted by worldly prelates – fitted the mood of 1918, not only on account of the horrors inflicted but because there seemed little to choose between the different war leaders and their aims. The discrimination in moral judgement which would become necessary in the case of Churchill and Hitler did not seem to apply to the men of 1914–18, all of whom seemed as ripe for debunking as their predecessors had been for being praised. The biographical atmosphere was quite different after the Second World War. Monsters like Hitler and Stalin did not need debunking; their actions put them beyond the pale; while a certain tone of piety seemed appropriate for those who, directly or indirectly, had saved us from their clutches.

The modern biographical mode is thus far from debunking: indeed, it has largely reverted to hero-worship, a hero-worship that shares much in common with Froude's since what used to be called the warts are often paraded now as evidence, and even causes, of the subject's exceptional stature. The idea of truth-telling has been transformed in other ways, too. It has been divorced from Strachey's passion for brevity and selection. Truth is equated with length, with 'telling all', with piling up detail on detail. It is ironic, at least, that those two exquisite miniaturists, Lytton Strachey and Harold Nicolson, should both have received the accolade of double-decker biographies. What one chiefly notices in modern biography is how professionally it is done, not that it is experimental in style or arrangement, or that it seriously challenges accepted judgements. Nearly all biographies still start with ancestors, move on to birth, and then through birth to leading events, and so on to death, in much the same way as of old, and at about as funereal a pace.

Ironically, it is the requirements of scholarship, as much as anything else, which tethers contemporary biography to its Victorian ancestor. Original sources mean, in practice, the subject's private papers; the widow means the person or persons who control access to, and quotation from, those papers. Thus the contractual basis of the Victorian biography, in which the widow granted the biographer access to family papers in return for his tact and discretion in their use, has been reinforced by the increased emphasis on 'original research'. There is also the prize to biographer and publisher alike for 'first use' of original material. This in practice means as soon after the death of the subject as possible, when the pressure to be complimentary is also highest. Strachey avoided the problem of the widow by using only published sources; his commitment to short biography was at any rate helped by his lack of energy, or commitment to what is now called serious research. The old idea that, with the telephone ousting the letter, biographies would be compulsorily slimmed through lack of material, has been shown to be quite wrong. In practice, more scholarly material than ever is being produced and stored. Private papers have become an important part of the estate of any dead person with a claim to fame, so that the incentive to preserve and even create material for posterity has been much enhanced. The danger now is not so much that biographers manipulate subjects who can no longer reply, but that subjects manipulate the evidence which they know their biographers will use. And institutions have become ever more gigantic producers and hoarders of paper. Of course most of this paper is much more boring than the conversation by letters which are the joy of biographies about Bloomsbury. But all that means is that the biographies of the future will be duller, not shorter.

Truth-telling in biography has thus been blocked off at many points: by the professionalism which increasingly makes biographies works of scholarship rather than of imagination, and segregates literary from political biography; by an intellectual *Zeitgeist* hostile to biography's 'central' justification as well as to the debunking mode pioneered by Strachey; by the biographer's continuing (and even expanding) relationship with the 'widow'; by the imprecision of the biographical aim. Although Strachey is much honoured as the father of modern biography, little, it seems to me, of the Stracheyean biographical programme has survived. What chiefly distinguishes the contemporary from the Victorian biography (apart from its greater professionalism) is its greater degree of explicitness about private life and its greater psychological penetration; neither of which, I think, were important aspects of Strachey's original programme. It is to these contemporary aspects of the truth-telling project that I now want to turn. By being unpardonably schematic, I can tell this story in three stages.

'Let us now praise famous men' (Ecclesiasticus 44:1). This is the familiar sentiment behind Victorian biography. Biographically worthy persons were those deserving of praise on account of their public benefactions – in action, thought or art. Their lives were written as models for emulation by prize-winning schoolchildren. Their characters and private affections were displayed as moral tales to emphasise the connection between virtue and achievement; when there was some glaring discrepancy – such as Nelson's love-affair with Lady Hamilton – it was simply concealed (by Southey in his classic life). It was what a person did rather than the life he led which was considered important.

Although the Victorians were obsessed by character, they were relatively incurious about motives, assuming those appropriate to the subject. One consequence of this was an ability to treat achievement in a fairly self-contained way. Victorian biographers and historians could depict dramatic events much more successfully than we can because they were untroubled by the thought that they were dealing with sublimated dramas. Biographers had no strong sense of the complexity of the links between private and public facts. Thus H. A. Taylor, in a standard Victorian-type life of Sir William Joynson-Hicks, which appeared in 1933, was not in the least bit curious about the possible private sources of the moralising zeal, already considered obsessive, with which his subject, as Home Secretary, prosecuted night clubs, prostitutes, D. H. Lawrence and Radclyffe Hall. Private life was dealt with in the standard sentence appropriate to such productions: 'But from the time of his marriage he had the real blessing of true happiness at home.'[8]

All this, of course, changed with Freud. The focus of post-Freudian biography was still on public achievement, the idea that the will to achieve is the sublimated expression of sexual drives, diverted from immediate gratification into tasks of culture and world improvement. The postulated link between high achievement and sexual repression not only provided a quasi-scientific endorsement of the Puritan character-type, but more obviously opened up private life, and particularly the circumstances and techniques of early upbringing, to biographical investigation.

Thus, long before the theme was turned into soap opera by Richard Attenborough, Gandhi's doctrine of non-violent resistance was traced by the neo-Freudian psychobiographer Erik Erikson to the 'feminine' way in which Gandhi nursed his sick father in order to 'deny the boyish wish to replace the (aging) father in the possession of the (young) mother'. Erikson continues 'Thus the pattern would be set for a style of leadership which can defeat a superior adversary only non-violently and with the express intent of saving him as well as those whom he oppressed.'[9] The difficulties of Freudian biography – particularly the use of the Oedipal conflict as the central explanatory tool – are too familiar to dwell on. The point is, though, that it identified efforts at truth with investigations of the subject's sexuality.

Two offshoots of the Freudian approach have been extremely

influential. The first is the postulated connection between sexual deviance and achievement. Empirically the case for this is quite strong – though we must bear in mind the possibility that our biographical sample is distorted by interest in sexual deviance *per se*. But it cannot be said that we have any very good theory on the matter – about how sexual deviance, or its stigmatisation as such by society, *causes* exceptional achievement, nor about whether or how it leaves its imprint on the subject's work – except in the relatively trivial case where a homosexual theme is being directly dealt with, as in E. M. Forster's posthumously published novel, *Maurice* (1971). I can't say I got much from the following passage from Leon Edel on Keynes: 'The accepting mother and the loved father committed Maynard's libido in two directions. . . . He is an exception to the 'Oedipal' – it had been dissolved.'[10] But the admitted fact that many exceptional people have been homosexual,[11] plus some neo-Freudian theorising on the matter, has chiefly served as a scholarly justification for introducing into biographies sexual material of a kind which before only used to come out in scandals and trials.

A second way in which Freudianism in its broadest sense has influenced biography has been in altering our conception of the nature and value of political activity. For Freud himself politics was one of the successful forms of sublimation. But this view was developed in the liberal epoch. The idea of politics as neurosis was adapted from Freud's theories by analysts like Wilhelm Reich specifically to explain Fascism and anti-semitism; and has since been extensively applied by American psychoanalysts like Bruno Bettelheim to all forms of political dissidence. In this guise it has not won wide acceptance from biographers. But it has undoubtedly led to the private dimension of political personality receiving much more attention than before; and has diminished our readiness to accept politicians at their own valuation as do-gooders.

The new emphasis on private life was not, of course, all the work of Freud. It also represented a coming to terms with a democratic age. By means of heaped-up personal detail, ranging from exploits of the breakfast table to those of the boudoir, a spurious mateyness could be established between reader and subject, far removed from the deference thought appropriate to contemplation of the deeds of Mr Gladstone or Mr Disraeli, over whose personal foibles (e.g. the former's propensity to self-flagellation) a veil was until quite recently drawn. This appeal to mateyness was a way of cutting leaders down to size, by making them seem much like the rest of us.

In that sense it represented a continuation of the debunking programme. But its motive was quite different from that of Strachey. It was not the rejection, but the celebration, of the commonplace that was being sought.

The great vice of what we may call Stage Two of modern biography is reductionism. Every achievement is actually 'something else' displaced and it is this something else which ought to be the focus of biography. The defect of this approach is that it ends up by one not having to take the achievement seriously – even though the achievement furnishes the actual 'claim to fame' of the biographical subject. It is hardly surprising that many writers have objected to having biographies written about them. They suspect that modern biographical methods are more likely to lead the reader away from their work than towards it. I confess to having a sympathy for this complaint. It is important to insist against the Freudians on the relative autonomy of achievement. Achievement should never be reduced to 'life and times'. Many scholars, literary critics in particular, would argue that this is impossible unless the life is dealt with in an entirely separate compartment from the work. This implies the abandonment of all attempts to make connections between the two, except those of a factual kind. I would not accept this. But some place in all decent biographies must be found for discussing achievement as expressive of a representative, not idiosyncratic, individual, that is as expressive of a tradition or style of thinking which can be discussed in its own terms.

This brings me to my Third and last Stage in the development (degeneration?) of the truth-telling programme. Humphrey Carpenter got round Auden's objection to having a biography written about him with an ingenious argument. While conceding that Auden's life throws no light on his poetry, he thinks that his poems may throw light on his life. This seems to me to amount to the proposition that Auden is worth writing a life of not because he was an important poet but because he was an interesting man.[12]

This represents a radical shift in perspective. It raises a basic question about the justification of biography. Let me illustrate what I mean. The foreground of Michael Holroyd's biography of Lytton Strachey (1967–8) is largely taken up with the private lives of Lytton Strachey and his circle. The truth-telling purpose comes out of what I have called the Stage Two of the biographical programme: 'I was setting out . . . to trace the effect [of Lytton's love-life] on his work'; or 'a knowledge of Lytton Strachey's life enables one, I believe, to read his books with new understanding.'[13] It may be that in Holroyd's life of Augustus John the justification has changed, the only explicit requirement now being that the subject 'must be stimulating . . . to the writer'.[14] Holroyd uses biography to alter the critical assessment of his subject's work. He is attracted to writers or artists whose stock is down. By the time he has finished with them, their stock stands higher. However explicit the treatment of private life, the justification of the biography is traditional: better to understand the subject's work.

In Stage Three, on the other hand, the criterion of biographical worth itself has shifted. We write biographies of people not because they achieved great or unusual things, but because they led interesting or unusual lives. Take the enormous quantity of words – words of high quality – which have been written about the lives and loves of Vita Sackville-West and Harold Nicolson. No one can say that the main interest in the life of Vita Sackville-West is the light it throws on her novels, which are now unreadable and unread: nor does Victoria Glendinning make this claim. The interest lies in her lesbianism, and more generally in the 'portrait of a marriage' which, it is suggested, might provide some kind of inspiration for our age.[15] As biographers we are once more in the business of writing exemplary lives. But now the example is the life itself, not what the life enabled the person to achieve. Or, more precisely, the life *is* the achievement; what used to be called the achievement is now only one accompaniment, possible a minor one, of a style of living. Quite obviously on this criterion a much wider range of lives is opened up to biography, paucity of achievement in the traditional sense being no barrier to being written about; conversely, some hitherto biography-worthy subjects might find themselves 'lifeless', because their (genuinely) blameless lives are no longer sufficiently exemplary to record; or because they imprudently failed to leave enough evidence of sexual or other unorthodoxy to make them suitable 'role models' for the next generation.

Biography is, as usual, following not leading fashion. The shift from Stage Two to Stage Three reflects the sensibility of our time, especially in its substitution of the democratic notion of 'fulfilment' for the aristocratic notion of 'achievement' as the criterion of biographical worth. The exemplary lives of our age are those that many look to to enlarge their possibilities of living; lives which might serve as models for groups like feminists who feel oppressed by the dominant social and sexual arrangements. But with the life, rather than the deeds, the achievement, we have entered new biographical territory, still largely unexplored.

Biographers write biography; they rarely spend much time thinking about how they ought to be writing it – at least not in this country. We have produced great biographers; but no important theorists of biography. Still, I have little doubt that our work as biographers would be improved if we were guided, though not dominated, by some theoretical conceptions.

This leads me to the first of the two suggestions which I would like to make. Practising biographers might consider, either for a subsequent occasion such as this, or in the introductions to their next biographies, writing an extended justification of biography as an intellectual enterprise – with the double purpose of clearing their own minds as to why they are writing biography at all, and of defending the biographical project against those scholars who claim that it is inherently distracting and trivialising. Unless this charge is effectively countered, biography will continue to lack a cogent scientific or imaginative justification.

My second suggestion is that biographers should be more audacious in their choice and treatment of subjects. We should try to break down the increasingly rigid demarcations between literary and historical/political biography. Literary biographers should be more ready to follow Lytton Strachey's example and write about men and women of action; historical biographers more prepared to write about thinkers, artists and writers. This, even more than a refusal to write 'official' biographies – my personal golden rule for all biographers – would help secure that independence of judgement which was central to Strachey's truth-telling programme.

The current segregation of biographical genres also needs to be questioned from another side. 'Serious' biography is still supposed to be about 'serious' people. This means that 'serious' biography ignores what is, in many ways, the dominant world of our time – that of entertainment. The entertainers – cinema and pop stars, pop artists and musicians, television and sporting personalities – are the distinctively representative people of our age. Yet we go on writing about politicians, soldiers, thinkers, and high-brow writers and artists as though these were the only suitable subjects for serious biography, leaving the entertainers to the showbiz and sporting journalists. Norman Mailer and Wilfrid Sheed are the only writers of reputation I know of who have attempted biographical studies of film stars and sportsmen. Yet as biographers we will surely have to define our attitude to this class of achievers. Are the 'personalities' in this world worth serious biographical attention? And if not, why not?

As to treatment, the time has surely come to protest against the tendency to identify biographical truth-telling with increasingly elaborate efforts to master the complexities of the individual case – efforts which have long been subject to the law of diminishing returns. There are two possible ways out of this particular cul-de-sac. Biographers might be more prepared, I think, to relate personality to type; to explore the typology of their subjects and not just their individuality. A successful use of this technique was by Nicholas Mosley who explicitly assimilated his father's life and actions to the categories of the classic drama: 'At the end of his life Tom [Oswald Mosley] was like Oedipus at Colonus – "beyond the pale" in the sense of his seeming to have broken some fundamental rule which had rendered him taboo.'[16] Outstanding people often appear to others as types, the originals of which lie scattered in folk memory, drama, fiction, even in the animal world. As Beatrice Webb put it the 'English are mostly dogs and birds – less often horses, cats and apes, but still fewer pigs'.[17] Not all of us *see* people that way. But a good biographical assumption would be that the law of independent limited variety applies as much to human as to animal and physical nature; and that simplifying techniques are both legitimate and necessary if we are to portray characters as they are actually perceived by others. Keynes might be seen as the type of the magician; it was thus that he saw himself, and thus that he was felt by others to be.

Another way of broadening the base of biography is to relate achievement to tradition. When we write biographies we should try to recapture not only our subjects' individual contributions but what John Dunn has called the 'intellectual present' in which they thought, wrote, and acted, the time when the past had happened, but not the future. We gain the freedom, thereby, to explore a much richer set of connections, and more persuasively, than those suggested by the simple division into 'life' and 'work'.

A biographer must be inspired by efforts at truth. But these can and must take the many forms appropriate to the subject. The current tendency to identify biographical truth with truth about individual lives is one aspect of the truth-telling programme, not necessarily the most important.

Notes

1. Quoted by Humphrey Carpenter, *W. H. Auden* (1981) p. xv.
2. Felix Frankfurter Papers, Reel 13, Library of Congress, USA.
3. Noel Annan, *Leslie Stephen* (1984) p. 56.
4. Lytton Strachey, *Portraits in Miniature* (1931) p. 199.
5. Lytton Strachey, *Eminent Victorians* (1918) preface *passim*.
6. See Michael Holroyd and Robert Skidelsky (eds), William Gerhardie, *God's Fifth Column* (1981) introduction, p. 18.
7. J. M. Keynes to G. Lytton Strachey, 21 February 1906; quoted by Robert Skidelsky, *John Maynard Keynes* (1983) p. 134.
8. H. A. Taylor, *Jix* (1933) p. 32.
9. Erik Erikson, *Gandhi's Truth* (1970) p. 45. This interpretation hinges on the assumption of an Oedipal conflict. Yet elsewhere Erikson acknowledges the irrelevance of the Oedipal conflict in India owing to the 'diffusion of the mother in the joint family' and therefore the lack of salience of her relationship with the father. (43).
10. Leon Edel, *Bloomsbury: A House of Lions* (1979) pp. 50–1.
11. In his introduction to *Homosexuality and English Literature 1890–1930* (1977) Jeffrey Meyers quotes a professor of English literature who remarked that 'it was really quite difficult to find any serious author in the last seventy years who was not involved with homosexuality one way or another'.
12. Humphrey Carpenter, *W. H. Auden* (1981) p. xvi. Carpenter seems to accept Auden's condition for writing the biography of a writer: 'provided that the biographer and his readers realise that such an account throws no light whatsoever upon the artist's work'.
13. Michael Holroyd, *Lytton Strachey* (2 vols, 1967–8) preface to the revised edition, pp. 20, 23.
14. Michael Holroyd, *Augustus John*, I (1974) p. xi.
15. See Victoria Glendinning, *Vita* (1985) preface, p. xviii. According to *The Observer* review, quoted on the cover, it was a 'biography that conceals nothing. . .'.
16. Nicholas Mosley, *Rules of the Game* (1982) p. 174. See the whole of ch. 18; cf. the chapter on 'The Faustian Riddle' in my *Oswald Mosley* (1981).
17. Norman and Jeanne MacKenzie (eds), *The Diary of Beatrice Webb*, IV (1985) p. 213.

2

Writing Lives

Ann Thwaite

The biographer is, first of all, a writer and must have the ability to tell a story. Though we spend a lot of time gathering facts, biographers are not primarily fact-gatherers. Certainly one reason I wrote my first biography was because I wanted to write. I *liked* telling stories, but was not convinced that I had anything much to say, in my own voice, that would beguile or even interest my readers. I was never at all sure when I wrote fiction that my imagination could invent plots that I would myself want to read. I always suspected, too, that any characters I might invent would be less interesting than real people. It was real life I was interested in. One of the pleasures of writing biography is that one doesn't have to choose, in any sense, between life and literature. One can have them both. The trouble with real people in everyday life is that we don't know them. We certainly don't know even our closest friends as well as we know Tom Jones or Elizabeth Bennett or Michael Henchard. We can't read their diaries or their letters – except the few they write to us, which often tell us far less than we want to know; and they often draw back when we ask them the really important questions. Our knowledge of the people around us is at best sketchy and partial. We have only our own view.

Of course, diaries and letters are not necessarily true. All evidence is suspect but – at least if we are lucky with the subject of our biographical attention – there is plenty of evidence. There are many different views. Librarians are happy to put before us hundreds, even thousands, of letters, written and received. There are glimpses in other people's memoirs and autobiographies; there are contemporary newspaper interviews. Among the mass of available evidence, it is usually the survivors' memories I find least valuable, especially when someone had been dead fifty years or so. The people that remember them have repeated their memories so often that, like the words in the children's game Chinese Whispers, they bear little real meaning.

17

I had a strong feeling that this was so when I talked to an old man called Harry Millum in the village of Rolvenden in Kent in 1971. His father had been a gardener. He himself had worked as a stable lad for Frances Hodgson Burnett, the subject of my first biography (*Waiting for the Party*, 1974) who was at that time playing out her dream of being the Lady of the Manor, at Maytham Hall. Harry was twelve in 1898 when she first took over the house and he earned half a crown a week. That much was fact. Over the years many people had asked him his memories of the famous author of *Little Lord Fauntleroy* and *The Secret Garden* (the Rose Garden at Maytham had long been identified, somewhat inaccurately, with 'the secret garden'), and he had often repeated a story about the gardeners at Maytham resenting the fact that she wanted to do their job for them, and about her writing in the Rose Garden 'as if she had something inside her she just had to get out'. It was only when I questioned him about Stephen Townesend, Frances's second husband, that I felt I was getting authentic evidence. No one, I am sure, had asked him about Townesend before, and the memories came out with a suggestion of truth. He thought more of his horse than of his wife, his stable lad told me seventy years later. Not long before her death in 1924, Frances Hodgson Burnett wrote to a friend: 'It goes to my heart to be told that Rolvenden remembers me kindly.' In 1971, sixty-four years after she left Rolvenden, I was moved to find how much she was still remembered by elderly villagers who had been children then.

Places are always important to the biographer. I try to find the houses where my subjects have lived. With Mrs Burnett, this was sometimes difficult, on both sides of the Atlantic, although David O. Selznick had put a plaque on the house in Washington where the 'deathless classic' *Little Lord Fauntleroy* was written, when he made the Freddie Bartholomew film version in 1936. I finally tracked down one of the Manchester houses she had lived in as a child and the City Council put a fine plaque on it, only to allow it to be demolished for road-widening a few years later. I also got a GLC plaque on the house, 63 Portland Place, London W1, where she had lived in the 1890s and had often entertained Henry James and Edmund Gosse.

Gosse himself had a less peripatetic life. I had a strange experience, when working on my second biography, in connection with the splendid London house where he had lived for twenty-six years until his death – 17, Hanover Terrace, Regent's Park. In 1901,

Gosse recorded that 'Mr John Belcher, ARA, is going to make some structural changes and put it fully into the modern state for us.' No further structural changes were made for eighty years. One Friday, early in 1981, driving into London as I rarely do (normally taking a train), I decided on an impulse that it would be a good day to have a look at 17, Hanover Terrace. I found the house covered in scaffolding with builders in occupation. By an odd coincidence I was just in time to see the house much as it had been in Gosse's day. It had been allowed to run down: the very next Monday it was to be totally gutted and renovated at vast expense. Yes, I could come in at my own risk. The builders' foreman had never heard of Gosse, but he entered into the spirit of my quest. 'Your chap would have touched that', he said, indicating a doorknob, 'That'll be gone on Monday.' I walked through the house alone, getting the feel of it, in spite of the builders' equipment that was everywhere, making sketches in a notebook, looking out of the upper windows. 'There is no view more beautiful than from our upper windows', Gosse had written in 1901. Eighty years later it was still beautiful, looking out over Regent's Park. For a moment, I felt particularly close to Gosse. He was indeed, as the builder had suggested, 'my chap' – though I could never really hope to understand the man whose character appeared even to Henry James, who saw so much of him, 'a baffling enigma'.

That phrase comes from a letter from James to W. E. Norris, at Yale. Leon Edel drew my attention to the fact that all James's most revealing comments on Edmund Gosse come from his correspondence with Norris. The biographer is, of course, always looking for these 'third person' remarks, and they are extremely difficult to track down in unpublished, unindexed letters. One can hardly read through all the letters from each of one's subject's friends, on the off-chance of coming across some comment on him. Inevitably one occasionally misses a relevant and revealing remark. The only two things I regret having omitted from *Waiting for the Party* come into this category. In a letter from James to Mrs Hugh Bell on 7 January 1892, he referred to Mrs Burnett as 'the rotund little Muse' and went on: 'She is a fatally deluded little woman, and I'm afraid cunning hands are plucking her of her downy plumage. I wish she would gather up her few remaining feathers while there is yet time and flutter them westward, where she has, after all, a husband and a child.' The second, less revealing reference is one that Mrs Burnett herself would have preferred. In a letter to Gosse on 2 February

1896, James considered the pall-bearers at Lord Leighton's funeral and said: 'When I am borne it must be by you and Norris and Arthur B. and Mrs Burnett: with the P. of W. well back.' Neither of these letters had been published when I wrote *Waiting for the Party*, and it was not surprising that I missed them in unindexed manuscript collections.

Working from manuscripts is, of course, much more fun than working from printed sources, however difficult the writing. One often has the feeling (at least *I* do, dealing with comparatively obscure people) that no one has been there before. I never know what I am going to find. There are few pleasures to compare with coming across something totally unexpected and revealing, such as in the Alexander Library at Rutgers University, some sad, unsigned lines in P. H. Gosse's familiar script, dated 4 April 1874, written after reading his son's early book of poems *On Viol and Flute*, or Edmund's own unpublished poem at Cambridge, 'Written the morning after our first child was born dead' – a sorrow, I think, he never referred to again. There may be some tedious hours in libraries: I would not deny it. But it is a very unusual day, in my experience, that does not add to my stock of rich material. My hand may ache (how I dislike writing in pencil), my head may ache, but I have very rarely been bored. I am always reluctant to finish work for the day – perhaps because I am usually trying to cram a fortnight's work into a week, to save on money and time away from home. Indeed, I have on many occasions, in those understaffed libraries which maddeningly close in the middle of the day, been locked in at lunch time. I think with particular pleasure of being locked in with Arthur Benson's diaries in the Pepys Library at Magdalene College, Cambridge, having to exercise enormous control so as to confine myself, among the four million or so words, to reading only the thousands about Gosse. Public record offices with their census returns, wills, certificates of birth, marriage and death – all these will reveal interesting facts. But they are on microfilm nowadays, and the real pleasures, as well as the real treasures, are to be found in libraries. It continually pleases me to think that, provided one has the right credentials, one can work in libraries all over the world without paying a single penny. It is always an acute pleasure to leave noisy Fifth Avenue, bound up the steps of the New York Public Library between the lions and, waving the right ticket (freely given), be admitted to the lovely silence of the Berg Collection; and, within minutes, to be reading letters to Edward Marsh, for instance, or the actual nasty words Virginia Woolf wrote in her diary about delightful Nellie Gosse seen as a black doormat.

There is a need for curiosity, of course. With both Frances Hodgson Burnett and Edmund Gosse, I felt extremely curious from the start. I couldn't believe in two particular published views of them. Marghanita Laski, in her study of three women writers for children (*Mrs Ewing, Mrs Molesworth, Mrs Hodgson Burnett*, 1950) called Mrs Burnett, as she emerges from a book by her son, 'aggressively domineering, offensively whimsical and abominably self-centred and conceited'. Could the author of *The Secret Garden*, I wondered, really have been so unattractive a character? Of Gosse, it was Virginia Woolf's words that surprised me. She called him 'a crafty, worldly, prim, astute little beast' and even 'a mean skunk'. How could such words describe the author of *Father and Son*? What sort of man had he become – the boy I left at the end of that book? Like H. G. Wells, like many other people, I wanted to know the end of the story.

There was a particularly personal response in me to the unflattering descriptions of these two writers, both, as it happens, born in 1849 and known quite well to each other, as I have suggested, in the literary London of the 1890s. *The Secret Garden* was one of my favourite books as a child. It is 'the most satisfying children's book I know', Miss Laski herself has written. *Father and Son* was also on my family bookshelves (along with a number of other books by Gosse, and Max Beerbohm's *The Poet's Corner* with its memorable images). I read *Father and Son* in a small green Heinemann edition when I was about seventeen and I know I liked it.

In my introduction to my *Edmund Gosse* (1984) I see I call *Father and Son* 'one of the formative books of my youth', but I fear this may be hindsight – that *at the time* it did not make quite as much of an impression on me as I would like to think. There is no certain way really of knowing the truth about anyone's past, not even one's own. We all rewrite history the whole time. I kept a diary when I was seventeen, but I can find no revealing passages dissecting the influence of *Father and Son*. Certainly it didn't encourage me into any confrontation with my parents, similar to the scene in the Gosses' orchid house. I continued to go quite happily to St Barnabas', Woodside Park. I do remember a series of small deceptions, designed to test how far I existed as a separate person: for instance, pretending I had done something I really hadn't, specifically to discover whether I would be found out. But the formative influence of *Father and Son* (like that of most of the books I was reading at the time, such as *Murder in the Cathedral*, *Nineteen Eighty-Four* and Elizabeth Taylor's *A Game of Hide and Seek*) was in fact simply to confirm me in the feeling that I wanted to learn to be a writer.

The spurs to write *Waiting for the Party* and *Edmund Gosse* did not come directly from *The Secret Garden* and *Father and Son*, or even from Marghanita Laski and Virginia Woolf. In each case there was, in between, a critic I respected. John Rowe Townsend, in the first version of his *Written for Children* (1965), drew my attention to the fact that so little had been written about Mrs Burnett. He also had an influence in turning me towards biography by seeming not to value my children's novel *The Camelthorn Papers* (1969) as much as I did. It was John Gross, in his *The Rise and Fall of the Man of Letters* (1969), who suggested that Edmund Gosse deserved a new biography. I am grateful to them for their suggestions. It is the modern biographer's main problem, it seems to me, that of finding someone worth writing about. Everyone has already been 'done'. I have no interest in writing the life of someone, even someone I am extremely interested in, where a recent biography already exists. I can see that biographers rarely say the last word, but it would still be impossible for me to write yet another life of Jane Austen or Charlotte Brontë, to tread on Robert Gittings's heels as Michael Millgate did so successfully with his 1983 life of Thomas Hardy, or to labour over Stevie Smith's papers as Frances Spalding is doing, while reading the reviews of the book on her by Barbera and McBrien.

As I have suggested, a lot of the excitement for me (and one needs excitement as well as the long hours of silent application) is in reading a letter which no one has read since the year, perhaps a hundred years ago, when it was first written and received. Of course it is convenient, and better for one's eyesight, if the letters are already published and annotated. A small proportion of Gosse's correspondence was in print: some of his exchanges with his American friends, his letters from Swinburne, his correspondence with Gide. But none of Mrs Burnett's letters had had this treatment and, working on my first biography, I constantly had the feeling, which I relished, that I was treading new ground.

There had been one biography before mine – the life I have already mentioned by her son, Vivian. It was published in 1927, three years after her death, under the off-putting title *The Romantick Lady*. I was very lucky to have this as a source book. It was practically unobtainable (had indeed never been published in England) and though it had been written in a fey style, it *was* strong on facts and surprisingly frank about most things, though understandably evasive about Mrs Burnett's long relationship with Stephen Townesend, whom, as I have said, she eventually married as her second husband. The Townesend family (great-nephews and so on) must have been saddened by some of my revelations about him (in particular, a very convincing indication of blackmail), after they had been so helpful to me. But a biographer has to learn not to worry excessively about the feelings of the living. I would never agree (and fortunately have never been asked) to submit a manuscript to the scrutiny of relatives. In the cases of both Mrs Burnett and Edmund Gosse, I did not approach the families, the literary executors, until after I had signed the contract with the publisher, so that they knew the book would be written anyway. The dread example of Lord Birkenhead's *Kipling* (1978) serves as a warning not to give in to the wishes of families. Philip Gosse, Edmund's son, gathering material for Evan Charteris's *The Life and Letters of Sir Edmund Gosse* (1931), suggested a sure recipe for an unsatisfactory biography when he wrote to Edward Marsh: 'You may be sure that every care will be taken that nothing is printed that can, in any way, cause annoyance to anyone.' Gosse himself detested whitewashing, and suggested the biographer should 'be as indiscreet as possible within the boundaries of taste and good feeling'.

I keep repeating to myself R. L. Stevenson's dictum: 'It must always be foul to tell what is false and it can never be safe to suppress what is true.' I base what I write on the evidence I have and write as carefully as I can about the trickier human relationships and situations. Mrs Burnett's daughter-in-law (Vivian's wife) was still alive, as a very old woman, when *Waiting for the Party* was published. It was a considerable pleasure to me to hear from *her* daughter how much they had both liked the book. Similarly I was nervous about Elfrida Manning's reactions to my account of her father's relationship with Gosse. She was the daughter of Hamo Thornycroft, the eminent Victorian sculptor, whom Edmund loved. It was to Thornycroft that Lytton Strachey referred when, asked whether Edmund Gosse was homosexual, he replied, 'No, but he's Hamo-sexual'. It was a great relief to me when Thornycroft's very elderly daughter told me she thought I had got the relationship right.

There is so much chance, of course, about what goes into a

biography and what doesn't, what has survived and what has not. The Gosse/Thornycroft letters are a case in point. I have found no trace of Thornycroft's letters to Gosse and must presume Gosse destroyed them (as he destroyed the most intimate of the letters of an earlier important friendship, with John Blaikie; as he destroyed so little else). But Gosse's own revealing, passionate letters, in his neat, legible hand, had been carefully preserved in Thornycroft's family. On our first meeting, Mrs Manning would not let me see them. She was working on them herself, using them for a study of her father's work: *Marble and Bronze: the Art and Life of Hamo Thornycroft* (1982). And she was obviously worried about what I might make of them – just as, years before, Mrs Burnett's family had been nervous about giving me the more sensational letters she had written to her son about Townesend. But I was not in a hurry. (Biographers should never be in a hurry; nor, of course, should they have any interest in rates of pay or financial rewards.) In the end, in both cases, the families trusted me sufficiently to hand the letters over with no stipulations about their use.

During the course of my work, Mrs Manning agreed to present Gosse's letters to her father to the Brotherton Collection at the University of Leeds, to join their great Gosse archive, including most of the letters Gosse had himself received during his long lifetime, the letters through which I read steadily from Lascelles Abercrombie right through to Israel Zangwill, over a period of several years. The letters to Thornycroft, which Mrs Manning had intended to leave to the Brotherton on her death, she gave in her lifetime, specifically to help me and on condition that the library photocopied them and provided me with a complete set of copies. It was a great help to have this large pile of letters actually in my study when I was writing the book. It was a helpful chronological guide (Gosse nearly always dated his letters meticulously, being a biographer himself) to so much else besides the progress and complications of the most important friendship of his life. But of course I would not wish for photocopies in my room of *every* letter my subject had written. That would be physically impossible – at least for someone like myself without the financial resources for, or indeed any compatibility with, microfilm.

It helps if one has some sense of what is going to be (or might be) useful, right from the very beginning. It helps if the subject has been dead for some time. I would never try to write a book about someone living. I prefer written, not spoken, evidence, as I have already suggested, and I could not cope with the problems of interviewing my own subject. I am full of admiration for Deirdre Bair, who had to perform the most extraordinary feats of memory when talking with Samuel Beckett. My own skills as an interviewer are limited. The recently dead are almost as great a problem. I am now working on A. A. Milne. When I talked to a connection of his, who was improbably the step-grandmother of both Mr and Mrs Christopher Robin, I found myself listening meekly to a reiterated 'But you can't put that in'. Stevenson's words I quoted earlier are a variation on Dr Johnson's advice to the biographer of the recently dead: 'It will be proper rather to say nothing that is false, than *all* that is true.' Such considerations are irksome for the biographer.

My actual working methods I evolved after an early conversation with Janet Dunbar, biographer of James Barrie, who happened to be near me in Richmond, where we were then living. She told me she used file cards in boxes for people, themes, book titles and so on, and dated A4 paper in ring files for chronological reference. It seemed to me to be a sensible system and I have used it ever since. So a selection of my 'R' files for Gosse contains Rackham, Arthur; both Raleighs, Sir Walter; Ralston, William R. S.; Reading aloud; Reading habits and tastes; Red Cross Committee (book sales during the Great War); Redesdale, Lord; Rees, Leonard; Reference habits; Religion (see also Churchgoing); Reputation (see also Fame); Respectability (see also Grundyism); Reviewing, his own (see also individual periodicals); Reviews, reactions to; Reynolds, Sir Joshua; Ribblesdale, Lord; Robins, Elizabeth, etc. etc.... In the end there were seventeen crammed file cards for Religion, for instance, and eight for Reputation. The chronological pages for a particular year could range in number from four to forty. Xerox copies of letters were also filed chronologically, but with numerous cross-references, of course, to file cards.

One of the problems of this method is that the file cards contain totally unchronological material – odd items gathered from different places at different times, as I happened to come across them. All the information I needed would be there, but it often took a great deal of further work, after I had stopped gathering material and had steeled myself to write something. I had to sort it all out before I could use it. To take a simple example, Gosse's cards on Illness or Servants or Cats, from being a jumble of quotations mainly from his own letters, eventually became an interesting chronological page or two, showing how much illness he had suffered in his life, and his relationships with his servants and his cats. The file cards on, for instance, Thomas Hardy and Henry James, required more complicated attention. First of all, I employed at intelligent typist (who eventually typed the whole book from my longhand) to sort out the dozens of references into a chronology and a pattern of themes – but it took her so many hours and cost me so much money (typists naturally earn a great deal more than biographers) that I had to abandon that method for the rest of Gosse's friends. I had to sort out everything myself. With A. C. Benson, for instance, one of the most complex and well-documented relationships of his life, I remember spending several days in a deck chair early in the summer of 1982, reading through everything I had noted on my cards, re-reading parts of David Newsome's biography *On the Edge of Paradise*, (1980) soaking myself in the material, trying to imagine Benson and sort out what he and Gosse really felt about each other.

When one has gathered material over many years, this 'reactivating' is a very important part of the process. I never write a word of the final narrative until I have stopped research. I think of my text very much as a narrative, a story, and indeed the letter I liked best of all the ones I had about *Edmund Gosse* was from a bookseller, before the book was actually published, telling me he had enjoyed the book as if it were a nineteenth-century novel. I like the equation: 'an ample narrative crowded with characters', in Humphrey Carpenter's phrase. To repeat: first come the years of research, then the ordering and soaking in my own material, then – when it is finally mastered – the rapid writing.

It is the middle stage that is the really hard work. It is at this stage one may become not builder but also architect, not craftsman only but perhaps (by some mysterious inexplicable process) also an artist. Dr Johnson was the first to claim biography as a distinct branch of creative literature. But Leon Edel has said that 'the imagination of form and structure' is 'the only imagination a biographer can be allowed'. No one wants a papier-mâché figure built of documents. It is the way that we use our documents that counts. And yet in the end, I believe, as Gosse himself did, that the form of a biography is less important than its content. The essential element is its actuality, its individuality. Reviewing Festing Jones's biography of Samuel Butler, Gosse relished the fact that Butler carried diarrhoea pills in the handle of his Gladstone bag when he went abroad, and bought himself a new wash-hand basin in 1887. 'These little things are my delight', Gosse wrote. They are mine too.

But of course the biographer must know a great deal more than he tells. There is as much skill in knowing what to leave out as what to put in. In 1927 Virginia Woolf wrote of the biographer: 'He [*sic*] chooses; he synthesises; in short he has ceased to be a chronicler; he has become an artist'. She changed her mind later on, as my old tutor Helen Gardner pointed out in her provocative presidential address to the Modern Humanities Research Association on 'Literary Biography' (1980). And I find myself inclining to accept their conclusions. I have a feeling that being a biographer is actually harder work than being a novelist or poet, but less exalted. We share with the creative writer the need for a *compulsion* to write, which carries us on when any sensible person would give up and concentrate on something with either financial or spiritual rewards – advertising, perhaps, or social work.

For there is not much justification for writing biography, pleasant as it is to add a little to the sum total of human knowledge, to feel one is passing on to the future scraps of information and some extremely good stories, which would otherwise be lost. The biographer needs to have a strong instinct for preservation. Gosse himself wrote to T. J. Wise in 1915 when working on his Swinburne biography: 'It is terrible news that Miss Watts has "thousands of letters"! I wish they would be burned in one great heap. The world is infinitely too full of such documents.' I can sympathise with Gosse's feelings, but I have never got to the stage of wishing for bonfires.

With Frances Hodgson Burnett, the archives were manageable. Somehow there remained just the right amount of interesting material to fill a reasonably sized biography. It was only 247 pages (half the size of *Edmund Gosse*) but it contained everything I wanted to put in. In fact, Mrs Burnett had an amazing life. I was extremely lucky that that was so. As Elizabeth Jane Howard said in her review, 'Mrs Thwaite is first to be congratulated on finding somebody so extraordinary and so neglected to write about.' I didn't feel it was exactly a reason for congratulation, but the more I worked on her, the more I realised how lucky I was to have found such a subject. It always surprises me that the feminists have not taken her up as a heroine. As a young woman, she supported her husband's medical studies in Paris with her writing. Some of her adult novels (including *That Lass o'Lowries*, recently back in print, I am glad to say, after nearly a hundred years) were remarkably unconventional, and she battled continually for a woman's right to live a life not dominated by men or children. There is a revealing reference in a letter Frances wrote, just after her second marriage, to her 'newborn bride' (*sic*).

I was lucky that the archives of Scribners, Mrs Burnett's American publishers, are so well organised, and I spent a happy week at Princeton working on them. I was also lucky that she was a playwright, that many of her novels had been turned into plays. This meant that there was a fat file of cuttings about her at the Lincoln Center, in the Library of Performing Arts. A comparison of the Acknowledgements in *Waiting for the Party* and *Edmund Gosse* tells its own story. For Mrs Burnett, most of the manuscript material came either from Princeton or from her own family. For Gosse, it came from literally dozens of different sources. There were very few references to Mrs Burnett in other people's books, but Gosse was always cropping up on the edge of other people's lives – as well as centrally, in Osbert Sitwell's *Noble Essences*, for instance. Roy Fuller sent me so many Gosse references from his own reading that at one point he dubbed himself 'Gosse Information Services.'

At times, when working on Edmund Gosse, I did feel over- whelmed by the sheer amount of material. I couldn't see how I would ever get through it, or (having, after many years, got through it) how I would ever be sufficiently in control of the material to write the book. I remember walking with my publisher, Tom Rosenthal, along the River Tas in Norfolk near my home and suggesting to him that I might do just *part* of Gosse's long life, perhaps from his coming to London up until his father's death – those were the years that interested me most. Tom was convincing that it was a definitive biography that was wanted; he didn't mind how long I took as long as it was a good book in the end. But how could I possibly come to terms with all those years of country house weekends, of *lords*, above all of Lord Haldane, whose numerous fat leather-bound volumes of letters (to and from), at that time still unread, appalled me every time I saw them, one side of the correspondence in Leeds, the other in Edinburgh? Above all, how could I rewrite *Father and Son*, that marvellous book which surely told everythingabout his childhood?

As it turned out, there was no real problem. The opening chapters of *Edmund Gosse*, far from rewriting *Father and Son*, are designed to be read alongside it. As for the House of Lords period, in the end I became as interested in that as in everything else. I had imagined Gosse's life might trail off as he aged and became 'stifled in roses'. But one of the things I came to admire most about him was his continued vitality – that he kept his zest for books and writing about them right up to the end of his life. In the month before he died, aged seventy-eight, he wrote three reviews for *The Sunday Times*. Even Virginia Woolf had to admire the way Gosse faced a dangerous operation rather than accept the life of an invalid. 'This kind of vitality always gets me', she wrote.

I remember several unhappy patches during my years of research on Gosse, always when I was not actually working, but contemplating how little I was doing and how much remained to be done. There were many periods when I could not devote myself entirely to the book, for different reasons. My own daughters were growing up. I had a continued involvement with children's books - an interest with which my first biography had obvious connections but *Edmund Gosse* none at all. At some points I thought I would never finish it. It seemed as if I had taken on something which, indeed, had no ending. And there were often discouraging reactions to the name 'Gosse'. Even at a Malcolm Bradbury party (a *literary* party, bearing no resemblance to the parties in *The History Man*), I met with blank looks. What was I doing? A biography of Edmund Gosse? No, they had never hear of him – one an English thriller-writer, the other an American scholar of contemporary fiction. I remember how much it meant to me when someone showed some real interest – Jonathan Raban, for instance, saying he was looking forward to it more then Crick's *Orwell*: 'We *know* about Orwell; we don't know about Gosse.'

When I was in the middle of actually writing *Edmund Gosse*, in the summer of 1982 – after nearly eight years of intermittent research and six months or so of soaking myself in the material – the sheer amount of paper threatened to overwhelm me. I made endless plans of sections and chapters with cross-references and different coloured pens. It seemed to me as if I was making an enormous jigsaw, but without the assurance that one has with jigsaws, that each piece has an inevitable place. I knew all along (as had not been so in *Waiting for the Party*) that thousands of pieces, even ones with interesting detail, would eventually have to be thrown away, not because they were not part of the picture but because the jigsaw was quite big enough without them.

I wrote very rapidly, often working for twelve or thirteen hours a day, even on Sundays. I totally abandoned my domestic responsibilities. I had the willing co-operation of my family, relieved that at last the mammoth task was approaching its end. I didn't care about anything but turning that mass of paper into a consecutive, readable story, into a book. 'A well-written life is much rarer that a well-spent one', André Maurois apparently said. If I was not going to have any life of my own (well-spent or not) that year, I would at least make as good a job of Gosse's life as I could. But the important thing, the only thing that really mattered, was to get it done. I will never be so mad, I thought, as to let myself in for all this hard work again. I started in May and I finished in September: 260 000 words in less than five months.

After the writing, there was the picture research and, at page proof stage, the index – the most tedious job of all, but one that I couldn't possibly delegate. And eventually it was published, and other things mattered – the reviews, the paperback, the long chance of a prize. With *Edmund Gosse* everything went well. And I forgot my resolution to concentrate on my own life in future, for my life had become the life of a biographer. The varied routines of researching into someone else's life had become a necessary part of my own life. I needed the treasure-hunt element, the feeling of always being on the lookout for something. I couldn't imagine life without long silent hours in the British Library reading room or the pleasure of taking out random books from the stacks in the London Library on the off-chance that the right name would be there in the index. I was even addicted to humping about the heavy decaying bound volumes of *The Times*.

So when Faber & Faber approached me, not long after *Gosse* was published, and suggested I might write the life of A. A. Milne, I was immediately interested. But this was a very different case. Milne died only in 1956. His son, the Christopher Robin of the books, is still alive. He has written his own story, and specifically said he wrote it because

> if I did nothing, then sooner or later someone would come and propose himself as my father's biographer. . . . To say No would be hard enough; but to say anything but No would be in the end to open my private world to a complete stranger and allow him to trample all over it.

After reading that, I decided that this time I could not accept the commission unless C. R. Milne accepted me as his father's biographer. I would not, of course, allow myself to be primarily concerned with his feelings, but I knew I needed his agreement.

There were other people who had wanted to write about A. A. Milne. His son had become used to saying 'No'. I am not at all sure why he agreed that I could do it, but, presumably, from the evidence of my two previous biographies, he trusts that I shall show a proper sensitivity (which does not imply a lack of candour) in my handling of the father/son theme which is at the core of A. A. Milne's life. I had coped with an important father/son relationship in *Edmund Gosse*, and there are obvious parallels between the experiences of Vivian Burnett and Christopher Robin Milne. Mrs Burnett's younger son was dogged all his life by his identification with his fictional counterpart. When he died in 1937 (aged sixty-one), the newspaper headlines read: 'ORIGINAL "FAUNTLEROY" DIES IN BOAT ... Vivian Burnett, Author's Son, who Devoted Life to Escaping "Sissified" Role, is Stricken at Helm'. Christopher Milne's life had been similarly affected. He actually wrote at one time that he felt his father had climbed to fame on his son's shoulders – that he had filched from him his good name and had left him with nothing but the empty fame of being his son.

It was not the fame that A. A. Milne himself had wanted. A few years before he died, he wrote a sad verse regretting how all his fifty years' work, his funny essays and plays, his short stories and novels, his serious treatment of the subject of pacifism, all 'would be almost lost' and only 'those four trifles for the young' remembered. When, not long ago, Dell issued his classic detective story – *The Red House Mystery* – in paperback, they subtitled it, inappropriately, as 'By the author of Winnie-the-Pooh'. How Milne would have hated that.

My own indignation is a measure of how much I am already identifying with Milne. I try to keep an objective attitude towards my subjects, but in practice I find, as I get to know them really well, I become more and more sympathetic. I feel particularly close to Edmund Gosse, poet *manqué*, biographer, family man, cat lover. I shared his feelings about friendship, and his longing to be liked. I sympathised particularly with his doubts that anyone would remember him after he was gone. (How amazed he would have been to discover *Father and Son* an A-level set book in the 1980s.) I found it moving as I worked on his papers to find his messages to me – his unknown biographer – his hopeful annotations and explanations. Evan Charteris never used his notes, for instance: 'My father was extremely tender with me about MJJ's death but he did not understand.'

Gosse obviously hoped that there would be someone in the future who *would* understand. I see it as the biographer's task above all to understand, in the way that a novelist obviously understands his characters, for he/she created them. It is only when we understand that we can write a biography that makes convincing sense as a story of one person's life. I accept entirely that, for all our contemporary concern with biography, the art of the biographer cannot justifiably be elevated to that of the writer who creates a work of literature out of his own imagination. There is no question that *The Golden Bowl* and *The Bostonians*, for example, are on a totally different plane (thinking of the word 'elevation') than Edel's life of Henry James (5 volumes, 1953–72). But of course I would much rather write a really good biography than a mediocre novel, and I would even go so far as to say that *most* biographers do a more impressive job than *most* poets and novelists.

If deconstruction rejects the historical, considering that all works of literature only exist in relation to the reader reading them now, then the biographer must be totally against deconstruction. He sees his subject – and his subject's writing if it is a literary biography – *in context*. The biographer will of course look at the subject's life with late twentieth century eyes, yet it is also essential for the biographer to see the subject in context, of how the life was as it was lived, of what his plays or essays, poems or stories meant to the people who read and saw them at the time, and what effect the writer and the work had on those who came after. A great deal depends on context. A letter beginning 'It has been raining all day' is not very interesting, but it would be if it were dated 3000 B.C. and signed Noah.

I am in fact glad to be concerned only with the lives of comparatively minor writers. Auden said, 'Good artists never make satisfactory heroes for novelists because their life stories are peripheral and less significant than their productions.' For the biographer the same problem arises, and the danger of using great novels to illuminate a life can produce its own distortions, as Helen Gardner pointed out in the lecture I mentioned earlier. In completely different ways, the lives of Frances Hodgson Burnett, Edmund Gosse and A. A. Milne were all *more* interesting that their productions. It seems to me a well-written biography should be worth reading whether the reader is particularly interested in the subject or not. Mrs Burnett, Gosse and Milne are hardly names to conjure with. They are in no sense stars – but their lives have enriched my own, and I am grateful to them.

3

Writing Political Biography
Kenneth O. Morgan

I may be writing here under somewhat false pretences, since I do not consider myself primarily a political biographer. On the other hand, I must confess that I have in my time written the biographies of three politicians, all very different – Christopher Addison (1980), Keir Hardie (1975) and David Lloyd George (1974) – apart from also editing Lloyd George's private letters to his first wife, Dame Margaret. I am also a voracious reader of political biographies written by others (including my distinguished fellow-writers), which may be an additional qualification! My main interest in political biography arises from my being basically an historian of political and social themes, in England, Wales and the United States above all, and here the role of particular individuals can have a considerable, often decisive impact. I am mainly concerned to use biography to try to answer political questions about public issues. Others may well be interested in political biography from the psychological, ethnographic or literary standpoints. In my case, I am a political biographer essentially because I am a political historian. In writing political biography, indeed, the emphasis on the private lives of major figures can often be much overdone and lead to massive distortions. Historically, they may be totally unimportant. The relentless emphasis on Lloyd George's sexual adventures – real or alleged – for example can lead to extreme misinterpretation of the career of one who was above all, night and day, a supremely committed politican, obsessed with the issues of the time. Nothing, not even sex, could or would interfere with that.

On the other hand, light shed on the private lives and personalities of politicians can also be highly relevant to the interpretation of their political outlook and activities. Again in the case of Lloyd George, for instance, the most interesting aspect of his relationship with the two main women in his life, – Dame Margaret, his first wife, and Frances Stevenson, his long-serving mistress and eventually his second wife – lies in the two facets of Lloyd George's personality and outlook that they illuminate. Dame Margaret brought out his abiding attachment to provincial Wales; Frances Stevenson symbolised his commitment to political life at the centre of power. Both are vital to an understanding of Lloyd George as a political animal. To take a different case, Keir Hardie's involvement with middle-class women in the suffragette or feminist movement of his time – especially with Sylvia Pankhurst, who was probably his mistress – is important not so much from the standpoint of their private relationship as because it added a vital personal dimension to Hardie's devotion to the women's movement. Some of his critics in the Labour Party from 1906 onwards accused him of concentrating more on feminism than on socialism. Perhaps here we have one of the main reasons for it.

The political biographer, in my view, should always keep his or her prime commitment to political analysis and explanation in full view, and focus attention accordingly. Asquith's liaison with Venetia Stanley, and all those remarkably frank letters written to her on matters of state just before and after the outbreak of war in 1914 are interesting above all because of the light they shed on Asquith's style as Prime Minister and the relationship of this to the downfall of British Liberalism. Ellen Wilkinson's affair with Herbert Morrison in the 1930s and 1940s, a remarkable aspect of Labour politics at the time, is most revealing for the personal complications it added to the Tribunite left in the Popular Front era, and the way it helped propel Ellen Wilkinson herself to a far more centrist or mainstream position. The fact that Morrison bitterly attacked Wilkinson's proposals to raise the school-leaving age to 15 within the Labour Cabinet in 1946–47 adds piquancy to their relationship, and perhaps puts it in perspective. Hugh Gaitskell's involvement with Mrs Anne Fleming, the right-wing wife of the author of the James Bond novels, when Gaitskell was leader of the Labour Party in the later 1950s, is significant not for its trivial personal content but for the light it brings to bear on the ethic of the Gaitskellite right and the roots of their revisionism of the socialist idea. In personal trivia, great political truths can often be unveiled, with devastating results at times.

The three biographies I have written concerned three very different personalities – Addison, Hardie and Lloyd George. Each of them perhaps sheds some light on the questions that the political biographer, in my opinion, ought to be answering, and I would like to examine each in turn.

Christopher Addison (whose career I studied in a book written jointly with my wife, Jane, and based primarily on her research) illustrates one important truth – the need to study the second-rank politicians as well as the titans. I am not sure that we have not learnt more from excellent recent biographies such as that of Austen Chamberlain by David Dutton (1986) or Ellen Wilkinson by Betty Vernon (1982), about the nature of twentieth-century British politics than from all the multi-volume epics on giants like Lloyd George, Winston Churchill or Ernest Bevin. Addison, without doubt, was not a front-rank politician. There was never any talk of him as a future Prime Minister – although if he had retained his Swindon seat in 1931 he would surely have been a central figure in the Labour opposition during the years of the National Government, almost certainly more central than the far more obscure Clement Attlee who did indeed rise without trace to the apex of power! But Addison was not a giant. He was a flat orator, and an uninspired writer (though his diaries retain their fascination for students of British politics during the First World War). His personality was prosaic and respectable; his married life was impeccable in its respectability. There were no skeletons in the good doctor's cupboard. Why, then, write at all about Dr Christopher Addison? Well, in my view, there are at least three justifications for writing his biography, most of which were, indeed, noted by reviewers of our book when it came out in 1980.

First of all, Christopher Addison, however dull or self-effacing in style, achieved great things. As the most eminent political doctor of the day, he was deeply involved in the debate over national insurance and public health in the years up to 1914. Thereby he helped open up a dramatic new vista of social reform and welfare. In the First World War, he was an important figure in several respects, first at the Munitions Department where he assisted Lloyd George in transforming the war economy and the system of industrial relations, and in producing those shells and weapons without which the war could not have been won. In the latter stages he was Minister of Reconstruction in 1917–18. He was thereby central to the Lloyd George government's plans (such as they were) for creating that 'land fit for heroes' so enticingly dangled before the credulous electors at the 'coupon election' in December 1918. After the war, Addison was the first Minister of Health in this country in 1919–21, and proved himself to be a significant social reformer. Apart from important new initiatives in areas of health and community welfare,

Addison also launched the first public-supported house-building programme in this country's history. For all the controversy over the inflated cost of building materials, 200 000 new houses were built by the local councils. A vital new principle of subsidised housing as an arm of national social policy was firmly established. Addison's career as a leading minister did not end here. After he joined the Labour Party as Minister of Agriculture in Ramsay MacDonald's second Labour government in 1930–31, Addison was a remarkably innovative and energetic minister. He began the broad system of marketing boards, price reviews and quotas for agricultural production which have transformed the life of the farmer over the past half century – at least, until the impact of the European Economic Community. Finally, Addison went to the Lords as leader of the upper House and served in that capacity throughout Attlee's six years as prime minister in 1945–51. He guided a stream of radical legislation through a hostile house and played his part in averting a possible constitutional crisis. Addison, then, had several spells in government office, all of crucial importance. He held major posts under Asquith, Lloyd George (in war and peace), MacDonald and Attlee, and left his mark on all of them, with permanent results. Addison indeed illustrates the truth that a little man can do mighty things, and invest an obscure personality with the aura of greatness.

Secondly, Addison is a major figure in British party politics. He was close to the centre of high political manoeuvrings at key moments in British twentieth-century history. In 1916 he was Lloyd George's main trouble-shooter and ally in the turmoil and divisions that afflicted the Liberal Party at that period. In the critical days of 1–9 December 1916 he took a major part in propelling Lloyd George to the premiership by mobilising substantial Liberal support in the House of Commons. Indeed, as a result of his efforts, over half the parliamentary Liberal Party emerged as supporters of Lloyd George rather than Asquith in this key confrontation. Thereafter, especially at the time of the 'coupon election' in 1918, Addison continued as perhaps the most important of Lloyd George's newly created party of 'Coalition Liberals' – the most important, simply because of his long personal association with the Prime Minister, and because Addison alone could supply a credible social policy which the new party desperately needed to retain its appeal and its Liberal credentials. Addison was also close to great events in July–August 1931. He was the only middle-class member of that minority of nine in the second Labour government which rejected MacDonald's proposals for a ten per cent cut in unemployment benefit. He was the first to propose that Britain should go off the gold standard. Addison was not the most important member of the minority of course – Arthur Henderson was the key figure within it. But he added weight and a reputation as a distinguished medical man and a long-serving and committed social reformer to the dissentients.

After 1945 he became as close to Clement Attlee as he had once been to David Lloyd George. They were neighbours in Buckinghamshire, since Chequers was near Addison's home in Radnage. Those weekend tea sessions between 'Clem' and 'Chris', where they and their wives easily discussed cricket and gardening no less than great events of the day, were important events in stabilising and reinvigorating the post-war Labour government. Time and again, as the surviving public and private records show (and as Lord Wilson once told us), Addison's great reputation in the Cabinet as a uniquely experienced minister and a personal confidant of Attlee, enabled him to intervene decisively in policy on health, food supplies, dominions relationships, defence, housing and much else besides. Few politicians have been so intimately bound up with great events and great crises over so long a period.

Finally, Addison is important for being prominent in the British progressive tradition, which, at least down to 1979, was the dominant strain in the modern history of British reform. He was a busy practitioner of the New Liberalism down to, and during, the First World War, straddling the late-Victorian liberal conscience with warm sympathy for the poor and the emergent labour movement. Twice he resigned over social policy; each time his resignation added something to British progressivism. In July 1921 he resigned courageously from Lloyd George's coalition government, over its failure to continue its public housing programme. In the event, it was the mighty Lloyd George, rather than the humble Addison, who was to suffer in the long run from the betrayal of the wartime pledges on behalf of social welfare. The Geddes Axe decapitated the Welshman as well. In August 1931, Addison – now a labour minister – resigned again, believing that a cut in unemployment benefit would be a savage blow to the health and living standards of the unemployed and the urban and rural poor. Again, a long-term renaissance was to result, in the wartime debates on social policy focusing on Beveridge and other blueprints, and in the welfare state launched by Addison and other ministers after 1945. Addison, by the circumstances of these two resignations quite as much as by his work as an executive minister, added vital impetus to a British reformist tradition. In his case it was always shaped by the controls and collectivism which he had witnessed during the First World War and which provided the framework for the positive state as he conceived. Addison, a second-rank politican, is a first-rank exhibit in the evolution of the main themes of British progressivism as it moved on from Liberalism to Labour. He also shows how a political biography can become the launching-pad of a far wider inquiry.

Keir Hardie is a very different kind of problem. There is no doubt about his charisma or central prominence. Indeed, one of the major difficulties for the biographer is to try to disentangle legend from reality. Hardie's legend is still obscured to this day by his folk-hero stature, and the image of 'cloth cap' incorruptibility. In fact, one of the initial points to be made about Hardie in a biography is that he was not at all a typical working man. Indeed, he did not even wear the cloth cap as usually understood by football supporters. When he turned up in Westminster in a horse-drawn wagon as member for West Ham South in August 1892, preceded by a cornet player playing the 'Marseillaise', he seems to have worn a deerstalker reminiscent of Sherlock Holmes. His headgear thereafter was distinctly Bohemian and romantic; after all, Keir Hardie was a contemporary of Wilde, Beardsley and the Yellow Book. Although he began life as a poor working miner in Scotland, and spent desperately hard years down the pit until he was twenty-three, he then moved on from that proletarian world to become a profes-sional propagandist or evangelist. His variations in dress – including a spectacular red tie, yellow trousers, purple muffler, sandals, a slouch hat from Philadelphia, even a Japanese kimono – suggest many things, but not a typical Scottish miner. His dress was as much misunderstood as was Michael Foot's donkey jacket. Hardie, like his friend Bruce Glasier, was an artist *manqué*, a Bohemian, an eccentric, 'queer Hardie', indeed, with an occasio-nally turbulent private life. He was a man who conformed to the romantic, perhaps Utopian, ethic embodied in the socialism of the Independent Labour Party as it unfolded in the 1890s. Beyond that, it is very difficult to get an impression of Hardie as a real human being at all, so frequently did his opponents traduce him as a demon, and his thousands of disciples exalt him as a messiah, even a latter-day Christ. When Hardie was howled down by a jingoistic mob in Aberdare in his own constituency in August 1914 when he attacked the war, he naturally compared his own sufferings to those of Christ at Gethsemane. With Hardie, as with another apparently saintly politician, Mahatma Gandhi, dealing with him in realistic political terms is peculiarly hard for his biographer. Yet the effort must be made, if Labour history is not to degenerate into hagiography.

A number of broad points may be made about writing Hardie's life which may be of more general interest. First, the source materials for Hardie exist in surprising abundance. Indeed, the huge quantities of correspondence with other labour leaders in Britain and overseas that I unearthed in various private places quite astonished me in the end. At the same time, this very bulk of material can be misleading. His voluminous letters with fellow socialists such as Bruce Glasier and Ramsay MacDonald, for instance, can be deceptive since his personal relations with both of them were difficult at times. Glasier in particular, despite his intense admiration for Hardie's gifts and charismatic appeal, was not above a kind of jealousy towards a socialist more effective and celebrated than himself. The biographer must always beware of the very existence of appealing and voluminous private material that may direct him towards erroneous interpretations of his subject. Plain spite is often a more effective stimulant to correspondence than are agreement or admiration. In any case, the main creative role of Keir Hardie as a pioneer of the labour movement is not illustrated primarily by his letters to and from parliamentary colleagues, or fellow leaders in the ILP or the Labour Party. His role in the labour movement is more directly reflected in the views of the inarticulate, often poor, even illiterate working-class socialists or trade union activists in obscure backstreets in industrial towns or mining villages. People like these, working-class men and women, without the archival resources or professional habits of their middle-class contemporaries, seldom leave records. Yet Hardie was their inspiration, even their God. The historian who tries to understand Hardie must not be unduly captivated or seduced by the fortunate mounds of attractive correspondence between celebrities. For him as for others, silence can be golden.

Secondly, the many facets of Hardie's decidedly strange personality must be sympathetically examined and understood by his biographer. Side by side with his urge for social justice and sexual equality, his passionate involvement with practical themes like unemployment or a minimum wage, was a mystical, prophetic

side. This came in many forms, for instance in the spiritualist
seances he held with the Salvationist, Frank Smith, or the way
Hardie's personality responded to the ethereal qualities of Indian
mysticism amongst the Hindus, Sikhs and Buddhists he encoun-
tered during his dramatic tour of India in 1907. Hardie's interest in
spiritualism was a real one: he even consulted a medium on how he
should vote on the 1893 Irish Home Rule Bill (the outer world cast its
ballot on behalf of Mr Gladstone). He also engaged in spiritualist
seances with young women socialists when he was a member for
Merthyr Tydfil in later life. Indeed one of them later recorded that
the spirit of Hardie revisited her in July 1945, thirty years after his
death, to give encouragement, and perhaps admonition, to the new
Labour government. Hardie's mystical, irrational side must be given
full play in explaining some facets, at least, of his personal rejection
of industrial, urban capitalism, and his Utopian commitment to a
different order of society, new Jerusalem indeed. In Hardie's case it
could also take the form of an exaltation of the Celtic qualities of his
native Scots – and even more the Welsh with whom he was bound
after being returned for Merthyr in 1900, at the expense of the
prosaic materialist outlook of the mere English. Hardie was indeed a
natural bard, in tune with the druidic fantasies of eisteddfodic
Welsh culture. This aspect of his personality tells one a great deal
about Keir Hardie. It also illuminates major features of the socialist
movement of his time.

  Thirdly, Hardie's internationalism should always be given due
weight. In a way scarcely conceivable in the insular, self-pitying
Britain of the 1980s, Hardie felt himself to be an internationalist, a
world socialist, a fraternal crusader for humanity. He felt himself to
be reinvoking the spirit of Burns, Wordsworth and the youthful
poetic enthusiasts for the revolution in France of 1789. He was
ceaselessly active in colonial liberation movements, in India above
all, but also in Egypt, Japan, the Straits Settlement – and amongst
the blacks in South Africa, where Hardie was one of the very few
visitors to detect the racial divisions and injustices that underlay the
new Union. This was at a time when a serious concern with foreign
or colonial peoples, other than a blanket rejection of 'imperialism' as
a concept, was almost unknown in the British labour movement.
Hardie also participated to the full in the Socialist International, and
became a close colleague of giants like Bebel, Jaurès, Adler and
Eugene Debs (he always insisted that America, too, had a glowing
socialist future). The biographer must try to penetrate the quality of

this internationalism, often ill-informed or sentimental, but genuine enough. He must try to understand how Hardie's long campaign for an international workers' strike against war had a genuine meaning for him before 1914. He must try to explore also how characteristic this kind of outlook really was of the labour movement of his time – and how influential, too, bearing in mind the way that all the Social Democratic parties of Europe, including the Labour Party, cast a majority vote for war and the national cause in 1914. Again, however, investigating Hardie's internationalism and world consciousness illustrates how political biography can be used to open up a wider area of inquiry.

Finally, the biographer of Hardie, as of all the great prophets and pioneers, must try to make some kind of imaginative leap beyond the formal records. How was it that this somewhat dour, often difficult man, a solid rather than an eloquent speaker, cast his personal spell over the British working class at such an early age? How was it that it endured, with Hardie's name surviving long after his death as a supreme symbol of honesty and incorruptibility? What nuances of language made his public speeches so unforgettable? He had a dignity and *gravitas* all his own. After all, he was but fifty-nine when he died, and a pretty worn-out fifty-nine too. Yet from his thirties, ever since his hopelessly abortive campaign in Mid-Lanark in 1888 when he polled but 600 votes, he projected his own unique image as 'Labour's grand old man'. Published memoirs can help a little here: Hugh Dalton's autobiography tells us how one self-confident, patrician undergraduate at King's, Cambridge, in 1907 was deeply moved by Hardie's courage in standing up to a howling student mob. Oral testimony can help too, both from eminent survivors such as Lord Brockway, who was swept into the socialist movement by Hardie's personality when he met him in 1907, and from humble party workers or trade unionists. Newspapers are also useful, especially the more obscure ones in industrial areas such as the West Riding of Yorkshire and south Wales. They illustrate the range of Hardie's exhausting activities and interests (not least the fact that he was a ceaselessly productive journalist and editor, among many other things). They also hint at the nature of the popular response to him. The correspondence column of very minor ILP or local newspapers can be a gold-mine here in presenting us with vital clues. But the final assessment lies in something that stands beyond the formal record, written or oral. Hardie could be variously assessed as an extremist or a kind of secular saint (if often a difficult or devious one). Against all the odds, he supplied a kind of inspiration, almost magic, that created a new political party and permanently transformed the nature of British politics. Men's minds might by swayed by the programmes and precepts of middle-class intellectuals like the Webbs or the Coles. But it took a Hardie – along with almost equally inspiring figures like Snowden, Lansbury and the erratic meteor of Victor Grayson – to capture their hearts and their souls. After several weighty biographies, this elusive quality of Hardie remains the enigma it always was.

Finally, let me turn to the massive figure of David Lloyd George, by any test one of the titans of the twentieth century. I have not, in fact, written a full biography of him (to do so adequately would be the work of many hands over several lifetimes). But I fear that between 1963 and 1982 I produced six books in which the words 'Lloyd George' appear in the title. So I may be deemed at least partially qualified to say something about him and the problems he poses for his biographer. At least eighty biographies of Lloyd George already exist, while Messrs Grigg, Gilbert, Cregier and W. R. P. George are currently engaged in multi-volume studies which are likely to occupy them and us for many years to come. One thing these enterprises show is that Lloyd George remains an enduringly fascinating figure for his would-be biographers. Another is the way in which the interpretations offered by historians and biographers have markedly changed over the generations. For many decades, from his downfall as Prime Minister in 1922 to the early 1960s, Lloyd George was a kind of universal scapegoat, denounced politically for splitting the Liberal Party and imperilling the unity of Labour and the Conservatives, erratic in his private life, a symbol of unreliability or mercurial dishonesty. Keynes's famous essay on his late colleague as a man 'rooted in nothing', projected in 'half-human' guise from the mists of Celtic antiquity, dominated the conventional wisdom. Since the mid-1960s, however, it is clear that Lloyd George has totally ceased to be a universal pariah. Indeed, almost all authors who now cover his career, including conspicuously John Grigg in his very fair-minded first three volumes, are broadly sympathetic to Lloyd George, even at times to the point of adulation. Lloyd George's stock has certainly risen sharply in the past two decades.

There are two possible explanations for this change in biographical fashion. The first is the emergence of new source material. The opening up of the Lloyd George Papers in the much-lamented

Beaverbrook library, directed in incomparable fashion by Mr A. J. P. Taylor, meant that from 1967 onwards a vast amount of material for Lloyd George's career, mainly for post-1916, was available to provide new assessments, or even answers, for puzzling aspects of his political life. (The Lloyd George Papers are now at the House of Lords Record Office.) The further opening up of Lloyd George's private papers in the National Library of Wales at Aberystwyth in 1972 added more detail for his earlier career in Wales prior to 1916. The very existence of these huge treasure troves naturally opened up a new Lloyd George industry of bustling scholars (of whom I was, indeed, one). Like all archives, they must be handled with caution. Nevertheless they launched new research and almost by their very nature implied a new regard or sympathy for Lloyd George, his objectives and his predicament. After all, before 1967 the case for Lloyd George had often gone by default. They also demolished many old myths, including one unfortunately perpetuated by Mr Taylor, no less, that 'Lloyd George had no friends and did not deserve any'. The volume of *Lloyd George Essays*, admirably edited by Mr Taylor himself in 1971, marked the turn of the tide in more ways than one.

In addition to new material, we also have the factor, I believe, of generational change. Many of Lloyd George's critics in the period from the 1920s to the 1960s, tended to be respectable middle-class Englishmen. Often they had been much involved in the downfall of the Liberal Party of which Lloyd George was widely regarded as the culprit. Since the mid-1960s, by contrast, younger historians, perhaps more in tune with an increasingly permissive era, certainly far more sceptical of the immutable permanence or self-evident perfection of age-old English institutions such as parliament, the civil service or the armed services, have looked on Lloyd George with a less jaundiced eye. Again, such recent themes as the enduring arguments over social welfare, over democratic accountability, over Ireland and world détente, have tended to shed a more sympathetic light on what Lloyd George was trying to achieve. It is new historians as well as new sources that have led to a change, to a Lloyd George created in the image of the contemporary world rather than in terms of the fading nostalgia of an imperial sunset.

A number of themes have particularly struck me in writing about Lloyd George and it is possible that they may be of more general interest.

First, I have always believed that the Welsh dimension to his career is of enduring importance. I first suggested this in a little book I published back in 1963; I suspect that more people agree with me now than did then. Lloyd George spoke Welsh fluently. His home was in Wales. His early political training was entirely in the context of Welsh politics, Welsh newspapers, Welsh chapels, bishops, lawyers, businessmen and labour leaders. He was but one of many gifted MPs from the Principality in the fin de siècle period. Down to 1906 he was supremely absorbed in the politics of his own nation, with disestablishment, tithe, church schools, land reform, temperance and modified devolution all part of the agenda. This was a glowing period of national achievement for Wales, politically, economically and culturally, and Lloyd George was both a part of it and responded to it to the full. Emotionally, he never left Wales. It is a critically important point that throughout his career, as his correspondence and much other historical evidence amply illustrates, he was a foreigner in English politics. He was the eternal outsider who always viewed the establishment and its institutions from beyond the pale.

Yet the second point, paradoxically, is that his Welshness can be overdone, or at least misunderstood. One can make too much of the Welsh background of Lloyd George, just as one can of the Corsican background of Napoleon – another provincial outsider who came to conquer a foreign world. In any event, Lloyd George's Welshness even in Wales was somewhat suspect. Long before he set up home with an English woman, Frances Stevenson, in Churt in the depths of Surrey, his position even within his own country was somewhat that of an outsider, too. He was, after all, detached from many of the main themes of contemporary Wales. He retained a fierce contempt for the puritanism and superstition of the chapels and the hypocritical respectability of the elders on the 'big seat'. He had scant interest in the campaign for public education which so dominated public life in Wales between 1886 and 1906 and which left the county schools and the University of Wales as its major legacies. Lloyd George, as a self-made man, whose education came solely from Llanystumdwy National School, did not respond as others did to the intellectual imperatives and social mobility that higher education could bring to an impoverished, remote country like Wales. Nor did he take a serious interest in Welsh cultural life, undergoing a massive renaissance in poetry, prose and academic scholarship in the period 1890–1914, with men like Sir John Morris-Jones and Sir Owen M. Edwards as its leading ornaments. Unlike other Welsh Liberals such as Tom Ellis or Llewelyn Williams, Lloyd George's nationalism was at bottom political (or perhaps socio-political) rather than cultural or linguistic. The Cymru Fydd crisis of 1896 (like devolution in 1979) showed how little that nationalism meant to industrial, cosmopolitan South Wales in reality.

Again, as with Keir Hardie, we must beware drawing too many easy conclusions from such of Lloyd George's letters as survive. His voluminous letters to his wife, Margaret, most prolific in the 1890s, naturally focus primarily upon Welsh themes and personalities since these would most naturally interest his wife back in her cosy world at Criccieth. The little Welsh catchphrases to sign off his letters would appeal to her, too. His letters to brother William, minding the solicitor's shop in Portmadoc and thereby keeping his brother's finances afloat, also naturally concentrate on local themes, including such matters as temperance or Welsh home rule which would engage William's attention. As Lloyd George relentlessly rose to the apex of public affairs in Westminster and on the world stage, his correspondence necessarily becomes more fragmentary – and his interests far more universal. The second ménage with Frances Stevenson shows how far Lloyd George by the 1920s had strayed, physically and emotionally, from his own land of Wales, even if he continued to exploit it for rhetorical purposes, 'Lloyd George's day' at the national eisteddfod included, to the end of his life.

There is another point, too, about Lloyd George's letters. It is well known that he was a casual, erratic correspondent. His letters often have a wooden, mechanical quality to them, with occasional fire as in his notes to his wife in July–August 1914 or his communications with Bonar Law and others in the supreme crisis of December 1916. On balance, Lloyd George's biographers would do well not to rely unduly on his letters as an historical source, fascinating though they may be. He relied more than most politicians on personal communication, face to face, either with individual 'responsive personalities' (perhaps press lords or self-made industrialists, perhaps foreign statesmen who appealed to him like Theodore Roosevelt, Briand, Maisky or – alas! on one brief occasion – Hitler), or else to mass audiences. He relied on personal contact to unearth vital information, to probe for individual strengths or weaknesses, or perhaps simply to express himself to the full. He was a beguiling talker – and an incomparable listener. No one was more skilled in disentangling the individual motives and prejudices of a delegation of church leaders, businessmen or trade unionists (who had open access to Downing Street in 1918–22 in a way unknown in MacDonald's governments). No one either was more adept, either with men or women (or, indeed, children for whom he had a special appeal) at 'charming a bird off a bough'. This suggests personal dimensions that private correspondence which somehow happens to have been preserved cannot reveal. Nor do newsreels or recorded broadcasts begin to convey this quality.

With these reservations always borne in mind, though, other major features of Lloyd George as a political leader do seem to present themselves to the historian, whatever his political or other inclination. Without doubt, he emerges as a supremely political animal, obsessed or fascinated by politics all hours of the day, with scant time for cultural or other recreation. Even his foreign travels had a powerfully practical side. On the other hand, he was a politician who always had wider objectives. it is impossible to read the records of Lloyd George's career without concluding that, self-centred and ruthless though he undoubtedly was, his career was fired by far more than simply personal ambition. In that sense, he is a far more interesting figure, and a more worthwhile one, than, say Lord Randolph Churchill as successive post-filial biographers have revealed him to us. From the outset of his career as an obscure back-bench MP from rural Wales – indeed well before he entered parliament at all – Lloyd George was a man fired by great animating objectives. The national interests and status of Wales; the radical reform and democratisation of the social structure of Edwardian Britain; the promotion of a vast programme of comprehensive welfare, progressive finance and collectivist reform; the reassessment of Britain's role in the international scene – these were his animating objectives well before 1914. People, parties and institutions that got in the way would be either cajoled or else crushed into submission. This belief of Lloyd George's that he embodied some kind of higher political synthesis that transcended mundane partisan issues like tariff reform, the House of Lords or the status of Ulster, reached a climax with his new role during the First World War, and his semi-presidential premiership that emerged from it. His rise to supreme power coincided with a series of fundamental transformations of British politics, culture and society since the turn of the century.

And yet, his peacetime premiership of 1918–22, launched when the British empire reached its greatest extent and Lloyd George himself appeared as the most dominating leader Britain had known since the time of Cromwell, also coincided with unmistakable signs of national weakness. Between 1918 and 1922, Britain underwent mass unemployment, an erosion of its financial and commercial primacy, a serious imperial setback in Ireland which presaged retreat elsewhere throughout the empire in the face of rising nationalism, a clear diminution of Britain's standing as a world power, including in naval terms. Lloyd George in the latter part of his career, indeed down to his last dramatic emergence in high politics during the fall of Neville Chamberlain in May 1940, was grappling with the forces of British decline. Some of his solutions proved transient and he never found an effective political instrument to promote them after October 1922. Like his Corsican predecessor, he finally met his Waterloo – in the unlikely locale of the Carlton Club. But here, too, a passionate absorption with supreme public issues, rather than purely personal considerations, dominates the career of this remarkable political figure.

The final aspect of Lloyd George's career which ought to engage his biographer lies in its perennial unorthodoxy. He was the quintessential populist. He always broke all the rules, at home, in chapel, in party politics, in Whitehall, in international peace conferences. However consistent his pursuit of a great abiding objective, he was always erratic, even wilful in methods. Such memorials as the Marconi case before the war or the Lloyd George fund and the sale of honours after 1918 testify to the dangers of this approach. He could indeed pay the ultimate price at the hands of the party regulars and the organisation men. Historians by their very nature and training, and perhaps by the placid, middle-class, professional world in which they commonly operate, are committed to the normal and the continuities of life. They reflect on great crises from the reassuring tranquillity of study or library, of glass or ivory tower. It takes a supreme effort of imagination – perhaps of will – to try to comprehend a man who by instinct and habit was a maverick and a rebel, with or without a cause. Throughout his career, there was a restless urge to take risks, to vault above and beyond the established political world of parties and the official machine. The First World War, with its dissolution of conventional party politics and its elevation of outsiders such as pressmen or business tycoons to centre stage saw Lloyd George truly in his element. The official Liberal Party, symbolised by Asquith, the aloof Balliol patrician, was part of the wreckage. British history after 1918 was in one sense a long reaction against Lloyd George and his methods, with the figures of Baldwin and MacDonald, the makers of the National Government in 1931, leading the outcry against him. As we have noted, it was an approach faithfully reflected in the history books until the mid-1960s.

The historian or political biographer should not moralise about this process, either way. He should regard himself neither as a hanging judge nor as an avenging angel. What he should rather try to do is to try to convey the essence of Lloyd George's rebelliousness, and his urge for dynamic change, the short cuts and sharp practice this sometimes meant, and the constant interaction between his dynamic, creative personality and a somewhat slower-moving world. 'Who can paint the chameleon?' asked Keynes of Lloyd George. Certainly there were aspects of the Welsh radical which remained irretrievably hidden from the fellow of King's, whose sympathy for politicians as a class (note his treatment of Woodrow Wilson, another patrician, for instance) was distinctly limited. Whoever succeeds in pinning down the chameleon-like Lloyd George in this way will go some way towards explaining the currents of British history in the first forty years of this century. He or she will also succeed in providing a supreme justification for political biography as an art form.

4

Lies and Silences

Victoria Glendinning

My title, or text, 'Lies and Silences', is borrowed from a novel by Penelope Lively, *According to Mark* (1985), one of two recent provocative novels – the other being Julian Barnes's *Flaubert's Parrot* (1985) – which play games with the relationship between fiction and fact. This is Penelope Lively: 'The novelist recounts as much of what happened as is appropriate or pertinent.... In other words, the silences of the novel are not lies but rejections of extraneous matter.' Later in the book her biographer hero envisages writing a biography in which any material he does not like will be simply omitted, in which 'the silences and rejected matter would be the appropriate silences and rejections of the novel.'

In fact this is what happens anyway, in the writing of biography. We do not have much choice about lies and silences. They accrue whether we will it or not. This is Julian Barnes: 'Books say: she did this because. Life says: she did this. Books is where things are explained to you. Life is where they aren't.... Books make sense of life. The only problem is that the lives they make sense of are other people's lives, never your own.'

I do not think when I am writing biography that I am saying, 'She did this because...', or only when I must. I believe only the most doggedly psychoanalytical biographers still want to explain the 'because' all the time, and they seem curiously dated, following their own free associations as often as not rather than the irretrievable associations of their subject. I believe we know, as any historian does, that history can deliver no final truth about motives or anything else. Some readers may seek for a final truth, and even find one – but that is their private adventure. All writers, whether of so-called fact or so-called fiction, are in the lies and silences business.

I would like to describe some of the ways in which biographers cannot help telling lies, and I hope that you will not feel that your intelligence is being insulted if I begin by reminding you of an old nursery-rhyme:

49

> Little Miss Muffet sat on a tuffet
> Eating her curds and whey.
> There came a big spider
> And sat down beside her
> And frightened Miss Muffet away.

What that is, or what it could be, is a fragment of Miss Muffet's biography, very much from Miss Muffet's point of view. Maybe she even wrote it herself. It illustrates one of the biographer's chief difficulties: the problem of perspective, or point of view. This is a problem for historians too, and scholarly historians spend a lot of their time thinking about the history of history and the validity of different models of thinking and writing about the past. The biographer's problems ar similar. Are you going to write someone's life as it appeared to that person – to Miss Muffet, say? Or are you going to take the perceptions and evidence of other people into account, which will change the picture a lot? If you are going to do that, then some research must be done on the Spider; what was his record, what were his real intentions, and did it all happen just as Miss Muffet said?

And are you going to try to give an account of the social and economic world that Miss Muffet belonged to? In that case you are going to have to find out about the tuffet on which she sat, and the provenance and significance of the curds and whey. In fact, if you look the rhyme up in the *Oxford Dictionary of Nursery Rhymes*, you will find a reference to the girl's father, Dr Thomas Moffat, an entomologist, who died in 1604. 'This rhyme provides entertaining material for speculation', remark the editors – i.e. for fiction.

This is a silly example, but it has served its purpose. Many of the serious biographer's problems are readily observable in the transactions of everyday life. Think only of this: if you go with friends to a party, and all agree to write down afterwards what happened at the party, the accounts will all be quite different. Each person will have had his own encounters and experiences, besides which each person has different attitudes, perceptions and prejudices. Also, most importantly, not everyone will tell the truth about what happened or did not happen to them that evening. Think too of what happens when two friends, or a married couple, have broken up. Listening to each in turn pouring out his or her dissatisfaction and resentment, the listener often just cannot put the two stories together. Each unhappy person is presenting a subjective view of events, and the question of which version is 'true' really has no meaning. The outsider, or biographer, may well have a third version or interpretation which would be rejected by both the interested parties.

Is the story of your life what happens to you, or what you feel happens to you, or what observers see happening to you?

The more you know about anything, the less easy it is to make definitive statements, let alone judgements, and indeed it is questionable whether moral judgements have any place at all in biography. Nevertheless it is the business of a biographer to produce a coherent text, narrative, discourse or thesis, however suggestive and impressionistic or however scholarly and impersonal she chooses to make it. If one only knows the outline facts about somebody (the amount I know about Cecil Rhodes, or Oliver Cromwell) it is relatively easy to trot them out with confidence – misplaced confidence. The botanist Linnaeus, writing in 1753 about the complex classification of roses, said that those people who had seen only very few kinds found roses much easier to identify than those who had examined many. It is the same with all knowledge. As I begin working on someone's life and work I pile up a great mass of material – contradictory, unrelated, puzzling. Most of my *a priori* suppositions go to the wall, and for a long and weary period of research no new model takes their place.

All the biographer's sources can mislead. What are those sources? Printed books, letters, diaries if one is lucky, other people's related researches and, if the subject is a modern person, the reminiscences of people still living.

Edith Sitwell, the poet, about whom I have written a book, had an unloving mother. Edith was not a pretty nor an easy child, and though the family lived in a great house in beautiful surroundings, Edith's youth, by her own written account, was ruined by her spoilt, pleasure-loving mother's attitude: disapproving, impatient, scornful, unpredictable and sometimes actually cruel to her awkward daughter. So much, one might think for Lady Ida Sitwell – until one remembers that she was virtually a child-bride, unenthusiastic about her husband, and probably appalled by pregnancy. Edith's younger brothers Osbert and Sacheverell became writers as well, and they, particularly Sachie, published copious memoirs about their mother. For Sachie she was beauty and softness incarnate, a vision of loveliness and security, indulgent and comforting. The two children, in the same family, had totally different experiences of the same woman. One can discount neither of them. Both are 'true'.

Perhaps we can trust diaries, unless they are too evidently written with publication in mind; though any diarist is bound to select, to present himself in one light or another even, or especially, to himself. Letters are even more problematic. They are written in different moods and for different purposes. A letter shot off in a foul temper to someone who has irritated you may not reflect your more permanent feelings about that person. All it proves is that the writer of the letter is capable of expressing foul temper. My guess would be that on the whole one is actually nicer and more affectionate in letters than one often feels – especially when writing letters of thanks or letters to someone who has influence in a field in which one wants to operate. The least obviously pleasant letters might be to those whom we know and trust best.

Vita Sackville-West wrote many thousands of letters to her husband Harold Nicolson, from whom she was often apart. These are nearly all letters of love, and if one saw no more of her correspondence than these, one would assume that the Nicolsons' marriage was a miracle of sustained romance – as in a sense it was, except that Vita was writing love-letters of a different kind to other people as well, nearly all the time. She herself summed up the biographer's problem over letters in the introduction to her edition of the diaries and letters of Lady Anne Clifford, one of her ancestors:

> We should ourselves be sorry to think that posterity should judge us by a patchwork of our letters, preserved by chance, independent of their context, written perhaps in a fit of despondency or irritation, divorced, above all, from the myriad little strands which colour and compose our peculiar existence, and which in their multiplicity, their variety and their triviality, are vivid to ourselves alone, uncommunicable, even to those nearest to us, sharing our daily life. . . . Still, within our limitations it is necessary to arrive at some conclusions, certain facts do emerge.

Certain facts do emerge, and certain patterns of behaviour and response. But the biographer will still make errors of which she will never even be aware. She has only the letters to which she is given access, or only those which have been preserved by chance or calculation. Many others may have been lost, or thrown away in sorrow, or from discretion, or just in a fit of spring-cleaning. The biographer is like a detective, following up clues and making connections, some of which will be false because of missing information. I have read a story about an old man in a Home who believed that geraniums ate bread at night, because he sprinkled crumbs over the geranium bed every evening, and the next day they had always disappeared. There was a piece of information, about birds, that he did not seem to have. Quite often a biographer, in good faith, must be making the Geranium Mistake.

Occasionally the lack of hard information of any kind is painfully obvious. We have learnt to beware of those biographies that are cluttered with sentences like 'Miss Muffet must have felt...' or, 'The Spider probably wondered...'. It is more satisfactory to acknowledge gaps in one's understanding, to face up to the silences, rather than to fill them with white noise or avoidable lies.

Letters, and the modern ease of access to photocopying machines, provide yet another trap. The biographer is so thrilled to have masses of original material that her book may turn out to be just a series of quotations from letters, linked by a commentary. I regret now the amount of direct quotation that I have included in my books about people. I suspect that the general reader, in any case, skips those little blocks of indented material in small print. Besides, it is a lazy option. A better way is to process the material, incorporating essential phrases and drawing conclusions, rather than serving up the ingredients of an argument or a narrative uncooked. Peter Ackroyd's *T. S. Eliot* (1984), which contains very little direct quotation mainly for the negative reason that he was not allowed to quote from all the copyright material, shows how suggestive and satisfactory it can be to do without. The subject's own voice must be heard; but there should be a qualitative difference between a biography and a volume of selected letters.

One trouble with the writing of biography is that the biographer is not a machine or computer, even though some biographers are using computers, and many more will be. The biographer brings to her task her own essential but dangerous imagination. Without imagination and intuition her portrait will be lifeless, but she should be careful not to novelise unintentionally, and not to project her own personality unknowingly on to her subject, in an act of identification, That, at least, is what I believe. I am a puritan in these matters. But it may be a vain hope to think that I am able or willing to keep the personalities apart. In Julian Barnes's novel, where the central figure is investigating the life of Flaubert and his own at the same time, he says: 'All biographers secretly want to annex and channel the sex-lives of their subjects. You must make your judgement on me as well as on Flaubert.' Books such as Richard Holmes's *Footsteps* (1985) show how interaction between biographer and subject can be exploited successfully, becoming indeed the true topic of the book.

An American academic, Ira Bruce Nadel, recently published a book called *Biography: Fact, Fiction and Form* (1985) in which he asks:

> To what extent is fact necessary in a biography? To what extent does it hinder the artistic and literary impulse of the biographer? To what degree does the biographer alter fact to fit his theme and pattern?

His view is that the biographer has every right to change facts in order to make a psychological or artistic point. This makes me shiver. He also believes in what I would see as the intrusion of the biographer, suggesting that 'discovery in biography now exists equally in what the biographer reveals about himself as well as what he uncovers about his subject.' It is probably true that compulsive biographers immerse themselves in other people's lives as a way of obliquely investigating their own; but this is the biographer's own business. Nadel's ego-trip is at one remove. If *Footsteps* were to become a model for all biographers, we should have to find a new word for the genre.

Yet you do get uniquely close to a person, studying full-time a career, a set of relationships and ideas, a family heritage, a social milieu. You do have to struggle to preserve detachment (if that is your aim), and neither to punish nor to be excessively partisan. You must 'reckon' your subject and be interested in the nature and value of what he achieved or was, or why is it worth all that work, or the reader's attention? Some biographers are natural hero-worshippers, seeing certain figures as above the common ruck in an almost religious way. Some people need to believe in heroes, just as others need to believe that though some have greater gifts or luck or drive no human being is in essence superior to his fellow-men.

The critic Desmond MacCarthy summed up the biographer's duty, and the fine line to be trodden between intuition and bare fact, when he wrote 'A biographer is an artist under oath.' That formulation satisfies my own aspiration. My unrealised ideal would be to write a biography that had the tension and entertainment value of a novel, using all and any narrative techniques, but including nothing that could not be backed up by documents or other evidence, and suppressing nothing of significance, however inconvenient it might be structurally or artistically. This makes biography a challenge, a sort of game.

The 'artist under oath' formulation rather suggests that the biographer is giving evidence before the bar of posterity, and that a judgement is going to be made by someone. Even if the biographer declines to make moral judgements, the reader is going to. We all finish the biography of a public figure with some idea of whether we like that person or not, whether we approve of his actions and attitudes or not, even if we picked up the book in the first place for information about his Acts of Parliament or literary career. Newspaper reviews of biographies often end up with a personal assessment of the subject, like a sort of character reference; and of course one of the purposes and pleasures of reading a biography is to assess, to weigh, to get a picture of a significant person in the context of his times. We like and dislike the people we meet in books as we like and dislike the people we meet in life.

In the past the lies of biography tended to be those of omission. When a great figure of the past century died, his life and letters, often in several volumes, were produced by a colleague, disciple, friend, or even a member of the family. Though some of the great classic biographies were written under this system, what went into them was severely censored. Material to the subject's discredit, professional and personal failures, misjudgements, and domestic black spots tended to be glossed over or omitted. The dreariest of these kinds of works read like an extended tombstone inscription; even the best make their subjects seem more noble and disinterested than we are likely to accept. It seemed the duty of the biographer not to be so much MacCarthy's 'artist under oath' as to provide a sanitized portrait, all skeletons firmly shut in the cupboard.

Now the wheel has gone full circle. Everything may be written about, and a biographer who chose not to grapple with significant sexual irregularities or crises in the personal life of her subject might well be mocked or reproached by anyone who knew, or later unearthed, the full story. It could be seen as whitewashing. Other peculiarities can be written about with equal candour – unreliability over money, or untruthfulness, or professional duplicity. The only reason now not to put something in is the decision not to hurt living people, or not to risk a libel action.

Lytton Strachey's *Eminent Victorians* (1918) is, famously, the first of the modern anti-reverential biographies, and the first of the modern biographies in which the art of imaginative writing was conspicuously exploited. Appositely, Michael Holroyd's life of Lytton Strachey (2 vols, 1967–8) is the paradigm for frank sexual revelation in contemporary biography. Holroyd's own claim is considerable:

> I was setting out to do something entirely new in biography, to give Lytton's love-life the same prominence in my book as it had in his career, and to treat the whole subject of homosexuality without any artificial veils of decorum.

In the twenty or so years since he wrote that book, the veils of decorum have been well and truly cast off and it has become possible to write candidly about any aspect of life. One result has been a growing gulf between the way professional academic historians write and the way biographers write. The historians grow more austere as the general biographer grows more intimate. And just as there was a sort of lie in the concealing, idealising biographies of the past, so there can be a more subtle sort of lie, because of trivialisation and a loss of proportion, in this concentration on the personal life. I feel that the wheel is turning again. Rupert Hart-Davis's biography of the novelist Hugh Walpole was published in 1956. Its author is a man of the world and a man of letters of the old school. He made no reference at all to Walpole's homosexuality. In 1956, this seemed like decent reticence, and the knowing could read between the lines if they chose. In the 1970s, when I first read the book, this descretion seemed to me like tiresome obfuscation, though I greatly admired the biography as a whole. It was reissued in 1985, and I re-read it. Now, the lack of explicitness seemed to me highly sophisticated. Walpole's sexual nature was self-evident. His Jamesian sexual recessiveness was reflected in Hart-Davis's decision. To have spelled out chapter and verse, and worse, would have distorted a delicate equilibrium. This is an extreme example, but I feel it is a pointer for the future. Meanwhile, Holroyd's decision to give his subject's love-life the same prominence as it had in his career seems to me a good working rule.

Writing about people who were themselves writers, as I have done, has its particular pitfalls. When, for example, a novel is generally known to be autobiographical, the situation becomes dangerous. Biographers may be artists under oath, but novelists are under no such oath. They are licensed liars, and writing a novel can have the same function as a wish-fulfillment dream, or a nightmare, taking elements out of real experience as so much raw material for the expansion of fantasy. Novels are sometimes written in an 'as if' or 'what if?' frame of mind, extrapolating from a situation in the writer's real life. Novels can tell you a great deal about an author, especially if you are already steeped in that author's way of thinking and feeling, but they can only be used very warily as biographical evidence. The danger is that you will serve up as hard fact what is in reality the creative lie of the novelist.

Another trouble about investigating a creative writer, as I have found, is that they have often prepared the ground, and laid down their own myth, by writing autobiography. Some autobiography tries to be honest, but at the very least a process of selection is involved, as with a diary; autobiography is likely to be nearly as much a work of art – i.e. a creative lie – as a novel. Rebecca West felt that her own life was like a 'bad book'; being an artist, and intolerant of bad books, she passed her old age revising history, giving chaos some form, revising the text of her life in order to make it tolerable.

How is the biographer going to check out what really happened? If her subject is a modern figure, she can go to the Survivors to hear their story, their version of events. The Survivors are at once the most valuable sources of information and the least reliable. You learn this when they themselves have written autobiographies, which you have read before meeting them. Books such as Stephen Spender's *World Within World* (1951), his account of his life in the 1920s and 1930s, is a good read and packed with useful pen-portraits of his distinguished elders and contemporaries. But these are measured, considered paragraphs; the accounts are not as frank as the anecdotes he might tell sitting around a table with friends. Naturally. But the great value of Survivors is that they are witnesses, with first-hand evidence of the events and scenes and personalities that the biographer is anxious to reconstruct.

For each of the modern literary biographies that I have undertaken I have been given, by my subject's family or executors, lists of people whom they suggested I should see – ranging from colleagues, friends and lovers to housekeepers, secretaries and distant relatives. It can be exciting in ways one could not have foreseen. When I was researching my book on the Anglo-Irish novelist Elizabeth Bowen, I had an invitation to visit a woman

scholar in Cambridge. I had no idea what connection she had with
Elizabeth Bowen. She told me that her late husband, a fairly well-
known academic, had had a love-affair with Elizabeth Bowen, and
she had in her possession some letters from Bowen to her husband.
Not only were they interesting as love-letters, but they were about
her writing, her reading and her general ideas. As we sat politely
over China tea and cake, the widow gave me a straight choice: I
could either quote from the letters, but suppress the name of the
lover, or I could say that Bowen had an affair with this man (giving
his name), but neither quote from nor see the letters. I chose to quote
from the letters, and conceal the identity of the lover, and in the
original hardback edition of my *Elizabeth Bowen* (1977) he is not
named.

This was a coup, in a small way; and it illustrates the value to a
biographer of following up all contacts, however unlikely, among
the Survivors. But it also illustrates the dangers. This distinguished
lady (who has since died) was not quite pure in her motives. She had
felt bitterly resentful, and had been made very unhappy by
Elizabeth Bowen's involvement with her husband, and she felt that
the letters she allowed me to see showed Elizabeth up in a bad light.

Most old and famous people, and those who have had famous
friends or relations now dead, are constantly approached for their
memories of the past. Some of them love it. Some of them do not;
they are understandably cagey, and maybe feel unconsciously sour
that their dead contemporary is getting so much attention, and not
themselves. Not all of them, like my Cambridge widow, are looking
for revenge. I have had spectacular help and gained valuable
insights from listening to my subjects' friends and relations. But
some will have axes to grind, or opinions that they want to impress
on the visitor. Sometimes their memories are bad, and they simply
remember events wrongly – think of the 'witnesses' remembering
John Reed in Warren Beatty's film *Reds*. If a Survivor had some
professional business, or an affair, or a row, with the biographer's
subject, he is naturally going to tell the story from his own point of
view. Seeing himself, rightly and naturally, at the centre of his own
story, a Survivor may overestimate his significance in someone
else's life.

Everyone has the right as well as the instinct to restructure his
own past. The contemplation of the past might otherwise be
unbearable. But some of the most blatant lies of biography may
come about through the biographer's uncritical reliance on any one

Survivor. At the moment I am writing the life of Rebecca West. Her illegitimate son Anthony West, now 70, is vehement both in person and in print about his mother's destructiveness and wickedness. I must listen to him very hard, and I have done; but his perceptions may have more to do with his own biography that with Rebecca's. He promulgates the Black Legend about her; there is also, from other sources, a Golden Legend. This, like all pathological situations, is a grotesque inflation of something we all know about ourselves. There is a nice 'me' and a horrible 'me' within the same personality, for everyone. The biographer, trying to make a synthesis of the many and conflicting aspects of a career and a personality, will end up causing offence to at least some of the Survivors. She must, in the end, forget the outside pressures and face her subject on her own.

She must hold on to a sense of history. No one would think of blaming someone in the long-distant past for thinking the earth was flat, or that the world was supported on the back of a tortoise, or for writing 'Here be Dragons' on a a map. We would not even blame repressive feudal barons for being feudal barons and having serfs; only the visionary and the genius can escape from the intellectual or social parameters of the age into which he is born. If you are not writing the life of a radical or a reformer, it is more than likely that your subject will have all the prejudices and superstitions of a particular group in a particular period.

If that period is 'history', we can accept it. When it is nearer to us in time, some attitudes seem intolerable to us. A biographer who finds, for example, that her English subject was, in the years before the Second World War, unashamedly anti-semitic, or arrogant towards the less privileged, cannot in the light of her own feeling and knowledge help feeling unease and distaste. Yet she cannot suppress the evidence of these now unacceptable attitudes. It would be no less foolish to suggest that such attitudes were an aberration, since she may well find that they were shared by a whole social class at the time. It must all be taken on the chin; but a sense of history should stop both writer and reader from condemning a single individual, when a social climate, or history itself, is both the culprit and the victim.

But one is forced, I feel, into writing bad history – or at least, provisional history – when writing about a modern figure. A historian gave me a wonderful image, which he thought came from Coleridge. I have searched for the reference without success, and if anyone knows it I would be glad if they would get in touch with me. The image is of the light behind the boat. We, in the boat, have a light shining on our wake, and we interpret the recent past by that light. But there is no light at the front of the boat; the future is in darkness. Our suppositions about the water behind us – about its depth, its dangers, and what is likely to lie below the surface – might be hugely modified if we knew what lay just ahead of us: a shelving beach, or rocks, or a thousand miles of empty ocean. Artists, statesmen, criminals, society figures, rebels, reformers, scholars, all look different for each generation, who see them in a different context – a context that contracts in relation to the receding and darkening past, and expands forward into new knowledge and mentalities. That is why every generation needs, as all commercial publishers know, a new biography of really major figures.

The essence of conventional biography is that one takes an individual out of the mass and sets him in a spotlight, fixes him in the arc of light behind the boat. Here the biographer is caught in a built-in lie. The spotlight effect – the total concentration on one person that biography exacts – throws all the peripheral characters into shadow. These secondary characters may be more significant in historical terms, but they can only be partially accounted for, in so far as they impinge on the subject's life. The result is distortion. The results of the further ripples are ignored, or imperceptible. It is false in the first place to take any one person as central in any scheme of things. To others she is but a feeble and distant ripple, and we are central only to ourselves. The biographer has to see events through her subject's eyes and through her own – an uncomfortable sort of double vision. But one cannot take on a whole society, a whole population, and still call it biography.

There are ingenious exceptions even to this, such as Hilary Spurling's recent book about the later life of Ivy Compton Burnett *Secrets of a Woman's Heart*, (1984). She had, in a sense, almost no material; the lady simply wrote her novels and had friends to tea and cucumber sandwiches in her flat. Hilary Spurling dealt with it in an Ivy-ish way by drawing in the life-stories of everyone Ivy met and knew, interspersing the network with apt quotations from the novels. It was inventive and it worked, and it is I think the classic exception that proves a rule.

The poet and critic Tom Paulin, reviewing Humphrey Carpenter's life of Auden, wrote that 'the great vice of the English tradition of biography is that it exalts the qualities of personal egotism and

eccentricity. . . . It makes its subjects less than human by humaniz-
ing them, listing their foibles and personal habits, and sweeping up
the detritus of lives.' But detritus becomes compost, with the
passing of time. The annalist technique of accumulating detail, as in
Hilary Spurling's book, has like all highly evolved devices its
triumphal aspect. But is there anywhere for the modern biographer
to walk between the daily littleness of her subject's life and the
inflation of that life into myth, which leads to author-theology?

I am disturbed by author-theology. It has to do, mostly, with
women writing about and around women writers of the past, who
take on an emblematic importance. They perhaps provide role
models for dissenting, aspiring modern women. In a society of
people who find the traditional religious framework useless for their
purposes, yet acknowledge the need and existence of some kind of
transcendence, the dead but immortal author seems to have the
answers. In becoming intimate with the inner life of, say, Virginia
Woolf through her letters and diaries, readers may feel they are
getting closer to the sources of creativity. The new gods of a minority
religion such as the Bloomsbury cult fight their star wars in the
pages of biographies: relationships, family trees, liaisons, rows,
couplings and sayings are recorded like those of the Greek or Roman
Pantheon. The sacred shrines – the homes of the gods when on
earth – are maintained, at some cost to the faithful.

The sanctified authors themselves become 'people in books', like
their fictional characters. Their lives are interpreted and reinter-
preted by priests of the cult, in the way that critics interpret and
reinterpret fictions. Virginia Woolf becomes no more and no less
real than her fictional Mrs Ramsay, herself a version, or vision, or
Virginia Woolf's real mother. The mirrors reflect back and forth.
There are heresies and orthodoxies, priests and bishops of the faith.
Books such and Lyndall Gordon's careful and sympathetic *Virginia
Woolf: A Writer's Life* (1984) can be seen as religious meditations,
rocking backwards and forwards between the Acts and the Word.
The religious analogy is not far-fetched. The Bishop of Durham has
faced the lies and silences, the creative fiction, of Christian theology;
and the life of Christ in its most familiar form is served up in four
consecutive separate biographies, not always tallying, the fourth
being something of a poetic gloss. Yet the Church is not in
institution that is noted for its experimental art.

We are all, as biographers, in the business of ancestor-worship,
even when we demystify and demythologise. The biographer is

distantly descended from those who recited long sagas about the illustrious dead to an audience around a fire in pre-literate days, to pass the dark evenings. Nowadays the lives written about may not be heroic. We may be more interested in social history, and in individual psychology, than in heroics. But the desire to tell and the desire to hear seem the same. Just why anyone wants to tell stories of past lives, and why, especially as people get older, they tell you they would rather read biography, for what it gives them, than fiction that is acknowledged as fiction, is a question to which perhaps someone will give me the answer. I think myself it may have something to do with the lies and silences at the heart not only of life-stories, but of life itself; something to do with the fact of life, by which I mean of course the fact of death.

5

Confessions of an Irish Revisionist

Ruth Dudley Edwards

In the more innocent days of 1964, Michael Flanders included in *A Song of Patriotic Prejudice* the lines:

> The Irishman now our contempt is beneath.
> He sleeps in his boots and he lies in his teeth.
> He blows up policemen, or so I have heard,
> And blames it on Cromwell and William the Third.

No doubt today that ditty would be banned in the London borough of Camden, now officially an Irish Joke Free Zone. A pity, for it is surely healthy that the English* should have the safety valve of laughing at the incomprehensible Paddy. (Unfair too, for Camden pubs and clubs resound nightly to Irish ballads designed to whip up racial hatred of the English. If the victims only had the wit to classify themselves as an ethnic minority, they could prosecute.) Flanders focused on one of those aspects of the Irish the English find most bizarre: their penchant for emotion about long-dead public figures. It should not really be surprising that a people who 'groaned under the Saxon yoke' from the twelfth to the twentieth centuries should take history personally, but the English have always been an unimaginative lot who could never understand the failure of those they governed to think like themselves.

It is quite possible for the man on the Clapham omnibus to have no strong opinions whatsoever on any characters in his country's

---

*I speak of the 'English' rather than the 'British', because the Irish have tended to regard the English rather than the Scots or the Welsh as their historic oppressors. Much is made in song and legend of 'Saxon Foes' and even the term 'Brit' is usually popular shorthand for 'English'. The twelfth-century conquerors of Ireland were Normans from Wales and the seventeenth-century Ulster colonisers were Scottish, so it is all rather tough on the English. It can be partially blamed on a woolly-minded pan-Celticism.

history. The Irishman-in-the-street, however, if he is over thirty-five, has had his head stuffed full of historical villains and heroes at home, at school and in the pub. His leaders have been reminding him throughout his life (depending on their political persuasion) that they are fired by immutable principles laid down by Wolfe Tone, Robert Emmet, Daniel O'Connell, Charles Stewart Parnell, Patrick Pearse, James Connolly, Michael Collins or Eamon de Valera, to name but a few. He will know that to accuse someone of behaving like Dermot MacMurrough (who in the twelfth century invited the Welsh invaders in to help him out of a little local difficulty) is a deadly insult. He will have been taught to boo or cheer at the very mention of any of dozens of names and no one will have confused him by suggesting that a baddy was kind to animals or a goody was slow to stand his round. What is more, he will have a genuine if superficial interest in all these people: even if he is not a reading man, he will probably scan any article in the local newspaper describing the time one or another of them visited Glocamorrah.

With that as background it should come as no surprise that historians – and even more so, biographers – can attract attention in Ireland in a way that would be unthinkable in the neighbouring island. Sometimes they even achieve notoriety. In Britain, celebrity for a biographer is to be invited to participate in literary quiz shows: in Ireland it is to be attacked publicly for misrepresentation, character assassination, tastelessness, disloyalty, or 'letting down our own'. More sophisticated critics use the work 'revisionist', which roughly means a jumped-up young Irish ingrate who is determined for careerist reasons to undermine all that the Irish hold most dear and have fought and died for down the generations. 'Revisionist' also means someone whose findings are politically motivated, as they fit in better with Garrett FitzGerald's rather than Charles J. Haughey's view of Irish history – a charge difficult to refute since Dr FitzGerald has read a great deal more history than has Mr Haughey.

In the last few years, the book which caused probably the greatest storm was broadcaster John Bowman's *De Valera and the Ulster Question* (1982), a work of impeccable scholarship which proved beyond a shadow of doubt that Mr Haughey was all wrong when he claimed (as he did frequently) that the founding father of Fianna Fail never considered compromising on Irish unity. Dr Bowman made a lot of enemies by revealing de Valera's doubts, inconsistencies and essential pragmatism about the north of Ireland: the extensive press coverage included an unconvincing anti-revisionist piece by an historian and close adviser of Mr Haughey's. However, though it is doubtful if many members of the Fianna Fail party have gone so far as to read the book, they have got the message. Over the past three years when they talk intransigently about a United Ireland, they have cited de Valera less and less. In a way which could not happen here, a biographer has had a direct impact on political debate.

I mention Dr Bowman out of fellow-feeling. In 1976 I published *Patrick Pearse: The Triumph of Failure* and achieved a similar notoriety. Virtually unknown in Britain, Pearse is in Ireland probably the most famous of all the dead heroes. He was an industrious man who made during his lifetime a small reputation as a journalist, poet, short-story writer and political polemicist. He was also a gifted and innovative teacher who ran his own school, and through hard work he became a great orator who specialised in revolutionary rhetoric. At the age of thirty-six he was proclaimed President of the Provisional Government of the Irish Republic and became nominal leader of the 1916 Easter Rising. He and his brother Willie were court-martialled and shot by the British Army.

The Rising had been highly unpopular, but the revulsion caused by the fifteen executions that followed it precipitated the 1918 electoral landslide of Sinn Fein, whose birth certificate, declared a contemporary, had been 'written with steel in the immortal blood of martyrs'. It was Pearse who achieved the greatest posthumous fame, and not only because of his leadership of the insurrection: there were his political writings, which by design lent themselves to quotation and rapidly assumed the status of Holy Writ; there was the twin tragedy of his and his only brother's deaths; there were the poignant poems he had written for his mother just before he died; there were the moving poems about him by Yeats and 'A. E.'; and his ex-pupil, secretary and friend, Desmond Ryan, published a popular and hagiographical biography in 1919.

When the politicians split over 1921 Anglo-Irish Treaty, Pearse was prayed in aid on both sides, but the anti-Treatyites quickly earned his *imprimatur*. There was no arguing with quotations like this one, taken out of context though they were:

We have no misgivings, no self-questionings. While others have been doubting, timorous, ill at ease, we have been serenely at peace with our consciences. . . . We called upon the names of the great confessors of our national faith, and all was well with us. Whatever soul-searchings there may be among Irish political parties now or hereafter, we go on in the calm certitude of having done the clear, clean, sheer thing. We have the strength and peace of mind of those who never compromise.

Even more potent was his mother's contribution. A simple, uneducated and emotional woman, she was ill-equipped to deal with the spotlight shone upon her as the most glorious of all Irish mothers. As a member of Dail Eireann she spoke against the Treaty:

> my first reason for doing so is on my sons' account. It has been said here that Padraig Pearse would have accepted this Treaty. I deny it, and on his account I will not accept it. Neither would his brother Willie accept it, because his brother was part and parcel of him. . . if I accepted that Treaty. . . . I feel in my heart. . . that the ghosts of my sons would haunt me.

Her blind support for de Valera led her to support the Republican side in the civil war and later his constitutional party – Fianna Fail. In consequence, her sons became in effect honorary posthumous party members.

The mawkish cult of Patrick Pearse developed apace. A 1932 biography by a credulous Breton described him as 'more than a patriot; he was a virtuous man. He possessed all the qualities which go to the making of a saint. . . it would not be astonishing if Pearse were canonised some day.' Some of his poems, stories and prose were put on the school curriculum, and teachers were formally instructed by the Department of Education to imbue pupils with his ideals. The history textbook in use in most schools described him as 'one of the noblest characters in Irish history'. In 1933, de Valera ended a broadcast to the United States with: ' "Ireland not free merely but Gaelic as well", wrote Padraig Pearse, who died before partition was effected. "Ireland not free and Gaelic merely but united also" – that is the objective of the Irish people today, and it will remain their unshakable resolve until it has been finally attained.' By the mid-1930s, Pearse's image was set in a mould from which it was not to emerge for 40 years. He was popularly perceived as a saint, martyr and devout Catholic whose death after the Easter Rising had overtones of Jesus Christ; he was a wonderful son and brother; a chaste man, he had had a pure romance with a young Irish-speaking maiden which ended in tragedy when she drowned trying to save the life of another; at the age of six on his knees he had sworn to free Ireland and he had devoted his whole life to that task. Veneration of him was to reach its highest point of absurdity in the early 1960s, when the Bishop of Galway adorned a side chapel in his new cathedral with twin mosaics of Patrick Pearse and John F. Kennedy.

Oddly enough, the only serious attempt to add some shade to Pearse's portrait was made by his first hagiographer, Desmond Ryan, a highly intelligent man who in maturity had had second thoughts. In a volume of memoirs, *Remembering Sion*, in 1934, although he wrote of him with love and admiration, he also admitted a darker side: his recklessness, his essential provincialism, his strong Napoleonic complex and his glorification of war for its own sake. The book was ignored.

Throughout the period I am describing, there was going on a quiet and inevitably slow revolution in the teaching and writing of Irish history, spearheaded by two young men who had taken their doctorates in London in the 1930s and had eschewed the traditionally partisan and sentimental approach to Irish history. Both became professors in Dublin – T. W. Moody in Trinity College, Dublin and his friend Robert Dudley Edwards, my father, in University College, Dublin. Many of their students became professional historians and there were striking advances in Irish historiography. This was to bear fruit in the schools in the vastly improved teaching of history and in a crop of new good textbooks in the 1970s.

The paucity of archives militated against serious work on the twentieth century, and when I graduated in 1964, although I wanted to do post-graduate research on Pearse, it proved to be impossible. His sister, Senator Margaret Pearse, was guardian of the Ark of the Covenant, and was not even prepared to admit that she had any family papers. With regret, for the sheer improbability of the Pearse myth greatly intrigued me, I had to find a more productive area of study.

When the fiftieth anniversary of the rising was officially commemorated in 1966, Pearse was represented in the media in the time-honoured way. Two biographical pieces of some substance were published. One was a slim paperback by Hedley McCay, who bravely alleged that Pearse suffered from a mother fixation and 'excessive religiosity', but since McCay relied on secondary sources and his own hunches, his book was easily discounted. The other – a serious essay by the gifted Dr David Thornley – proved disappointing. Thornley, a romantic man who became a disenchanted politician, had fallen under Pearse's sway, and the only real criticism he made was to admit that his subject lacked a sense of humour.

There were some new developments in the early 1970s, not least a growing acceptance in the Republic that despite all the political rhetoric Ireland was manifestly not now, or likely in the foreseeable future to become, either Gaelic or united. Another historian and politician, Dr Conor Cruise O'Brien, rounded on the purveyors of nationalist mythology and lost his Dail seat for his pains. But in questioning, *inter alia*, the moral validity of 1916 he opened the door to public debate. His views were similar to those of Father Francis Shaw, who in 1966 had written an article called 'The Canon of Irish History – a Challenge' which he was unable to have published until 1972. In this he pointed out correctly that contemporary Irishmen were taught to 'despise as unmanly those of their own country who preferred to solve problems, if possible, by peaceful rather than by violent means'. He venomously denounced Pearse, accusing him of having been possessed by a blood-lust.

Father Shaw was so intemperate in his assault that he won few converts, but unlikely allies were coming to his aid. Sinn Fein were causing some unease by busily kidnapping Patrick Pearse from his long-standing owners in Fianna Fail. He was quoted and pictured on the literature they sold outside the General Post Office in Dublin in which he had spent Easter Week. And soldiers from the British Army in Northern Ireland came to assume that his photograph on a mantlepiece signified that the home was occupied by 'Fenian bastards'. Few southern nationalists supported the IRA, and one of Yeats's poems took on a worrying new relevance:

> Some had no thought of victory
> But had gone out to die
> That Ireland's mind be greater,
> Her heart mount up on high;
> And yet who knows what's yet to come?
> For Patrick Pearse had said
> That in every generation
> Must Ireland's blood be shed.

In certain jaundiced Dublin circles Pearse began to be talked of as a megalomaniac and a psychopath. Some muck-rakers went back to his poetry, read lines about the ruby red lips of young boys and concluded that he had been buggering his pupils.

It was around this time that an alert young editor at Victor Gollancz Ltd decided to commission a biography of Pearse. My name was suggested by an Irish adviser who knew of my long-standing interest. Though I had been settled in England for several years by then and was working in telecommunications, I could not resist the commission.

I could read secondary sources in London, but it became necessary in 1975 for me to return temporarily to Dublin and work on the project full-time. I was advised strongly by most of the experts I consulted that I was attempting the impossible. Their arguments were varied and impressive. There were those who pointed out that in the limited period I had available I would not even be able to read Pearse's countless newspaper articles: no one, for instance, had ever read through the six years of the weekly paper he edited. Then there was the language problem: a significant amount of the primary and secondary source material was in Irish, and mine was rusty in the extreme. I was assured that two if not three other biographies were in preparation and I would be left behind in the race. It was confidently asserted that in any event it would never be possible to get at the truth since so much material had been suppressed. And said some, since I clearly did not like him, I was the wrong person to write his biography. (That I did not take seriously, as I had long since been indoctrinated by my father into believing that objectivity was the greatest virtue and one that I possessed.)

I was worried by the amount of material which had come to light in the previous few years as the 1916 generation died off. They now included piles of unclassified papers discovered after the recent death of Margaret Pearse. It was obvious that what had been envisaged as a short biography largely based on secondary sources should instead become a substantial book involving a massive amount of primary research. Despite real fears that I would be pipped at the post I went ahead for a variety of reasons: I am tenacious by disposition; the British civil service, who had offered me a job, agreed graciously that they could do without me for longer than we had agreed; my father robustly dismissed the warnings as absurd; my mother, a scholar of the Irish language, was positively

eager to translate everything I needed; the man who later became
my husband volunteered himself for all the time-consuming leg-
work of material collection; and of course I could not afford to repay
the advance.

The typescript which I carried to London in November 1975, two
days before I became a civil servant, revealed a tortured and
complex man who bore little relation to any of the current views of
him. That he was totally sincere, selfless, kind, generous and brave,
both physically and morally, was beyond doubt. He was certainly
deeply religious, but obsessed with Calvary and much given to
images that identified him with the crucified Christ. He was a loving
son and brother, though one might question whether he did either
his mother or brother a favour by leading the unworldly Willie
Pearse to his death. He was not only chaste, but so innocent that he
betrayed again and again his latent homosexuality. (As for the tragic
romance: the girl existed and she did drown but everything else
about the story was invented.) He was also financially irresponsible
was perpetually being saved by friends from bankruptcy. Although
he was always genuinely devoted to serving his country, he
frequently changed his mind on the priorities (for many years the
Irish language and educational reform topped his list); indeed he
was a proponent of constitutional Home Rule only two years before
he led a revolution. His vanity prevented him from ever questioning
his own judgement, and he was so lacking in understanding of his
fellow men that it was my conclusion that he 'wrote, acted and died
for a people that did not exist'. His naïvety was such as to make
nonsense of his reputation as a serious political thinker. Take this
quote from April 1916:

> In a free Ireland there will be work for all the men and women of
> the nation. Gracious and useful rural industries will supplement
> an improved agriculture. The population will expand in a century
> to twenty millions; it may even in time go up to thirty millions.
> Towns will be spacious and beautiful. . . but, since the country
> will chiefly rely on its wealth and agriculture and rural industry,
> there will be no Glasgows or Pittsburghs. . . . Literature and art
> will flourish. . . The voice of a people that has been dumb for many
> centuries will be heard anew; and it will make such music as has
> not been heard since Greece spoke the morning song of the free
> people.

It was a combination of what Yeats once described during Pearse's lifetime as his 'vertigo of self-sacrifice' and his despair at having failed to achieve any of his ambitions that drove him towards martyrdom. Determined on immortality, he sought and found it in the only way he could (hence the book's subtitle: 'The Triumph of Failure'). To ensure that his name would be blessed down the generations, he left behind him a carefully constructed self-justificatory political testament that turned out to be a Pandora's Box. The methods of the IRA would have appalled him, but the gunmen were his natural heirs.

Having become fond of and sorry for Patrick Pearse and having taken the precaution of having the typescript criticised by people whose judgement I trusted, I was confident that the book was fair. I knew it would upset a lot of people in both camps by demonstrating that he was a human being, but even so, I was completely taken aback at the interest it excited. Once the review copies went out and word went round, I began to get phone calls from Dublin asking for interviews. Irish television decided to devote a whole political programme to the book's implications for Irish attitudes to 1916. I had to take an unscheduled week's holiday from my vain attempts in Whitehall to halt the decline of British manufacturing industry. On the day of publication, just before I left for Ireland, I was interviewed by Irish radio for the lunch-time news. To my chagrin, the questions were largely about Pearse's sexual inclinations.

The first three reviews appeared together, the day after publication, in a weekly Irish journal called *Hibernia*, which had enterprisingly asked Lord Longford, Enoch Powell and a daughter of the executed 1916 leader, James Connolly, to give their various views. Longford, a close friend and great admirer of de Valera, was clearly troubled by the book, but with his usual honesty and kindness he gave me credit for trying to be fair. Powell managed to denounce Pearse and 1916 on the evidence of the book without ever mentioning it. Nora Connolly O'Brien appeared to have read only the first chapter and provided a rehash of the stock myth, right down to Pearse's broken heart after his fiancée's death. The same night the television programme based on the book showed about one minute of an interview with me and then turned into a rarefied theoretical dispute between academics about Irish identity. It would all have been dscouraging if it had not been so funny. Irish radio made amends with a serious interview; Irish television featured me and three members of my family and jokes were cracked about us being 'The poor man's Longfords'. The litterati came to the rescue in ensuing days with amazingly good reviews, but some of them almost induced in me an attack of paranoia. Dr Conor Cruise O'Brien, although he clearly thought I had been rather wet in dealing with the 'baneful' effects of the Pearse legacy, approved in the main. This approval, he explained, would probably 'form part of the indictment' against me and he spoke ominously of how parts of the book would be considered 'blasphemous'. Sean O'Faolain gave me a rave review in *The Guardian*, but concluded that I would not be thanked for dissolving 'the golden icon'. Others spoke of my courage, and one newspaper interview with me had the headline: 'RUTH UNMOVED BY THE CONTROVERSY NOW RAGING AROUND HER NEW BOOK'. After a week of heady publicity I returned to London rather relieved not to have been knee-capped by a maddened patriot. I left Pearse behind me in Dublin climbing up the non-fiction best-seller list. By a wonderful irony, he made it to no. 1 by out-stripping *Roots, Jesus of Nazareth* and Galbraith's *The Age of Uncertainty*. On my next visit a few strangers wrung my hand in public houses and I received only compliments. Apart from a couple of rude letters I experienced no hostility. Media interest tailed off and I concluded that the ominous predictions had been normal Irish exaggeration.

Over the next couple of years, however, there were several telling incidents that reminded me that middle-class Dublin was not representative of the Irish people. One was the sympathy my mother was proffered by a nun claiming distant kinship, who hoped she was bearing up despite the shame I had brought on the family. Another followed a lecture I gave not long after I had presented an hour-long television documentary on his life. A stream of people (mainly young, for, encouragingly, the better-taught younger generation seemed unworried by the truth) came up to me afterwards to shake my hand and congratulate me. As I put out my hand to what I took to be another well-wisher, she put both of hers on her hips and said: 'I've come from the Aran Islands to tell you that the people there will never forgive you for your belittling of Pearse.' Yet a third followed a lecture at a summer school in the west of Ireland, when a priest, pointing to a group of teenagers in the audience, asked me in genuine distress what I would put in the moral vacuum left now that 'you've taken Patrick Pearse away from them'. And then there was the unperformed play about Pearse that I picked up in a bookshop, sporting a preface in which my biography was described as

grossly marred by a tendentiously hostile commentary which
seems intent on belittling Pearse in his personal as well as in his
public life, by insidious innuendo as well as by blatant
disapproval. . . . [It] is a typical example of the cynically revisionist
school of Irish history which has blossomed in the fertile ground
of the trauma resulting from the renewal of sectarian and political
violence in Northern Ireland over the past decade.

Rather worrying too was the way my admirers kept harping on my
courage – a quality I had never known I needed when I wrote the
book. I came to realise that they believed that I had made enemies
who would somehow wreak vengeance on me or my family. There
is a warning phrase in common use in Ireland – usually of parish
priests – that 'If he doesn't get you, he'll get your thirty-first cousin'.
Well, 'he' didn't, but in recent years it has dawned on me that if I had
been working in Ireland in a vulnerable job things might have been
different. I know for instance of a teacher who was sacked for
writing a distinguished novel that was considered by a priest to be a
dirty book. And more recently, a fine broadcaster of the wrong
political persuasion had to be denied a promised job when there was
a sudden change of government.

At no stage had there been a squeak out of the Fianna Fail party,
despite what I had said in the book and on television about their
exploitation of the myth of Pearse. They were in government in the
year of his centenary and I felt for them in their embarrassment:
between me and the IRA, they were on a very sticky wicket. Their
solution reflected the eminent good sense of their then leader, that
honourable pragmatist, Jack Lynch. Money was provided for a
Patrick Pearse pageant; there was a Pearse stamp; his decayed
school premises were refurbished; and there were other commem-
orative odds and ends. Grass-roots proposals for a statue of the
great man were quietly buried. Ministers could not avoid having to
speak about him on occasion at public functions, so they talked
boringly and at length about his remarkable gifts as an educationa-
list. Anyone ignorant about Pearse would have been hard put to
gather from ministerial pronouncements that he had ever left the
school premises. The only remark of a political nature that I can
remember being made was a pathetic statement from one minister
that Pearse would have been an enthusiastic supporter of the EEC.

Not long after his hundredth birthday, Pearse virtually disappeared out of political rhetoric. Even some Sinn Fein leaders must

have read the book, for increasingly they placed their emphasis on other martyrs. I can take some credit for having achieved the opposite of what biographers usually do. I wrote about someone famous and succeeded in plunging him into public obscurity. He has been virtually abandoned to the historians. (Honesty compels me to admit that he still has his fans among the non-reading public. I recently heard an Irish group called the Wolfe Tones singing in a Kilburn club the ballad they launched in 1979 – 'A Tribute to Patrick Pearse'. The chorus goes thus:

> The poet and the Irish rebel
> A Gaelic scholar and a Visionary
> We gave to him no fitting tribute
> When Ireland's at peace only that can be
> When Ireland's a nation united and free.

Somewhat nettled by the sight of about 2000 young, second-generation immigrants cheering and clapping an inflammatory song about a man of whom they had probably scarcely heard, I enquired of the Wolfe Tone who had composed it if he had read my biography. He was very polite: he did not call me a revisionist. But he explained that he had read some of it and thought there had been no call for me to put in the negative bits.)

Dr Bowman's equally dubious achievement has been to remove President de Valera – as far as the North is concerned – out of the arsenal of Fianna Fail. Both of us have the satisfaction of having made a contribution to bringing Ireland further out of what has been called a 'necrocracy'. The men of 1916 no longer have much of a role as formulators of the policies of modern constitutional parties. Even Sinn Fein, who need dead patriots to exploit, are getting up to date by creating new ones. Perhaps the next sensational biography will be a truthful one about Bobby Sands.

6

The Art of Biography
Robert Blake

The fact that a person has written a biography or even two or three biographies, does not necessarily mean that he can discourse with any competence on the 'art of biography'. Indeed, I have in the past tended to avoid that subject. Arguably one might write better biographies by not thinking too much or too self-consciously about the correct way of doing it. There is always the danger of the centipede who, you will recall

> was happy quite
> Until the Toad in fun
> Said 'Pray which leg goes after which?'
> She lay distracted in the ditch
> Considering how to run.

If one thought too much about the pitfalls, snags, and traps which lie in wait for the biographer one might never set pen to paper at all.

However, the composing of this chapter has been a challenge. It has made me think about matters which had not occurred to me before and caused me at least to try to see the process of biography in some sort of perspective. The first point that I would make is that made by A. O. J. Cockshut in his very illuminating study of nineteenth-century biography entitled *Truth to Life* (1974), and this is the neglect of biography as a form of literary art. There have been countless analyses of the novel as an art form – and it is true that the two centuries since the publication of *Tom Jones* in 1749 have been the golden age of the English novel. But it is also true that roughly the same period has seen the golden age of English biography. If one is to be precise over dates, the great era of biography began slightly later than that of the novel – with Dr Johnson's *Lives of the Poets*, the first four volumes appearing in 1779. And Dr Johnson has a double association with its origin. If his *Lives* represent one end of the biographical artistic spectrum – the short condensed pen-portrait, then surely his own *Life* by Boswell (2 volumes, 1791) represents the other; and that is the extended full-scale 'official' or 'authorised' biography based on letters and documents – and in Boswell's case on intimate personal knowledge. Many people have attempted this genre, but Boswell's achievement remains in the judgement of most critics not only unsurpassed, but unequalled. Whatever one's opinion of Boswell, the fact remains that a great British biographical tradition stems down from then onwards and is with us still. As modern evidence are the lives of Virginia Woolf by Quentin Bell, Charlotte Brontë by Winifred Gerin, the Duke of Wellington by Elizabeth Longford – and many others beside.

The reason for the neglect of biography as a form of literary art is, therefore, not any lack of good examples in the English language. It is, I suspect, something different – the difficulty of deciding just what a biography is supposed to do, and hence the difficulty of establishing standards by which a biography can be measured. For a biography is doing or should be doing at least two things. One is to give a record of the historical facts. Biographies in that sense are works of reference and unless they are accurate, get the person's date of birth right, mention his principal achievements, say who the subject married and tell us when he or she died, they are of no use. An accurate biography may be dull and lifeless. It may be the sort of work which, as someone said of a book by a friend of mine, 'when you put it down it is very difficult to pick up again'. But if it is correct and accurate it has at least achieved something. A biography which is incorrect and inaccurate might be lively, well written, moving, entertaining, elegant and so on, but its inaccuracy rules it out as a biography. It may be in one sense a work displaying literary art, but the critic must condemn it for it fails to do the first thing which every biography must do, namely: get the facts right in so far as this is possible and not make them up when this is impossible.

Of this latter defect, I would like to quote an example. One of the most entertaining books of biographical studies is Lytton Strachey's *Eminent Victorians*. When it came out in 1918 it seemed a marvellous contrast to the rather stuffy long-winded 'life and letters' type of biography which had hitherto commemorated – almost entombed – some of its subjects. General Gordon, Cardinal Manning, Florence Nightingale, Dr Arnold – what fun it was to see them in their true colours and not through the eyes of devout panegyrists! But was one really seeing them in their true colours? Lytton Strachey said that Dr Arnold's legs were too short for his body. Challenged as to his evidence he cheerfully replied that he had none – merely his conviction that Dr Arnold was the sort of man whose legs would be too short for his body. Another example is the entirely fictitious conversation that he invents between Archdeacon Manning and Pius IX in which the Pope holds out the appeal of high promotion to a potential convert. We know from reliable sources that Manning was an ambitious man. But there is no need to suggest that he went over to Rome because Pius IX personally tempted him with a hint of a cardinal's hat – which is in any case highly unlikely.

I do not wish to condemn all Strachey's efforts. His life of Queen Victoria in 1921 is remarkably good and the much larger amount of material made available since he wrote has largely confirmed his surmises. Lady Longford pays tribute to this in her own *Victoria R.I.* (1964). Nevertheless, he was, for all his brilliance, glitter, irony and wit, an unsound biographer: he was concerned with effect rather than truth.

Yet it is clearly not enough for a biography to be simply a correct record. The original edition of the *Dictionary of National Biography* (20 volumes, 1882–1901), that great product of late Victorian earnestness, represents in condensed form just that ideal which had also been aimed at in the extended form of a host of grave multi-volume works published during the nineteenth century about particular individuals. Many of these works were attempts to make the facts speak for themselves, or the story to tell itself without the interpolation of the author. But in reality the facts do not speak for themselves. A biographer who tries to avoid interpreting them is abdicating from his central task. It may be difficult to make such an interpretation. It may be the case that two (or even more) interpretations are possible. What is sure to kill a biography is to make no interpretation at all. As Professor Cockshut puts it, 'Books written by authors who were uncertain of what they really thought of their subject, or afraid to say, are quickly forgotten.'

The problem of interpretation is not at all easy. In a sense any biographer starts with some sort of interpretation in his mind before he begins to look at the mass of material which constitutes his sources of information. It is not wrong to have a preconceived notion about one's subject. If one had no ideas at all about the person one would probably never embark on the task. What is wrong is to allow the preconceptions to colour one's actual use of evidence. Alternatively – and less damagingly – a biographer may be so reluctant to let go of his preconceptions and yet so honest and reluctant to suppress the evidence against them that his picture becomes self-contradictory. The interpretation simply will not fit the evidence.

The classic instance of this (cited by Professor Cockshut) is Froude's picture of Henry VIII in his *History of England* (12 volumes, 1856–70). Froude was convinced that the Reformation was one of the most glorious events in English history, and he correctly saw that it would not have happened but for Henry VIII – or at any rate it would not have taken the particular form that it did but for him. Froude, however, was not able or willing to see that the course of history can be determined favourably in some circumstances by persons of an odious moral character, just as it can be determined unfavourably in other circumstances by persons of good character. The influence of Charles I and Henry VIII illustrate both sides of the coin.

The result of Froude's version, for he was an honest historian over the facts and documents, is that his picture of Henry becomes increasingly at variance with the supporting evidence which he produces, but which in the end ceases to support. The reader is left in a curious state of confusion. The work is wonderfully readable. It carries one on from page to page with increasing interest. Yet there is something about it which fails to carry conviction. In the end the evidence produced shows that the interpretation is wrong. Henry VIII was not a man whose defects were those of exuberant youth and whose later crimes can be explained away by the fearful strains of autocratic rule over a precarious kingdom in a precarious era. He was a ruthless monster, a Stalin, not a Churchill or a de Gaulle.

I had something of a problem of interpretation when I wrote my biography of Disraeli which was published in 1966. I chose the subject because there was a gap to be filled. No one had written a serious book based on his papers since Monypenny and Buckle's six-volume 'official' biography, which came out between 1910 and 1920, and I had always been fascinated by Disraeli's career and personality. But my picture of him, my interpretation, changed as I worked on his papers.

I suppose I came to them with a preconception which went roughly thus: Disraeli was a man of genius who made his way from humble and obscure origin, fighting against a barrage of prejudice, spite and malice. He had great determination and courage, and he had a Tory philosophy, a sort of Tory radicalism or democracy which it was his ambition to put into effect. Because this was incompatible with the rather arid pragmatism of Peel, Disraeli regarded it as his duty to overthrow his leader even if he could not stop the repeal of the Corn Laws. The result was long years of opposition until in 1867 he 'educated' his party into the virtues of democracy and conferred the vote on the urban working class. The reward was delayed and he lost the election of 1868 – but it was reaped in 1874, and as Prime Minister for six years he was able both to enact a major series of measures of social reform at home and to give a new emphasis abroad to Britain's (or, as he would have said, England's) role as a great imperial power.

But as I studied his papers, his speeches, his writings, his whole career, I began to have doubts about this interpretation. To begin with, it soon seemed clear to me that his origins were by no means as humble and obscure as all that. One had only to look at the beautiful red brick Queen Anne House which his father, Isaac, rented for the last twenty years of his life – Bradenham Manor near West Wycombe in Buckinghamshire – to see that his background must have been at least comfortable. Isaac Disraeli far from being obscure was a well-known literary figure. It appears to have been only accident that prevented Benjamin going to Winchester where both his younger brothers were educated. Jews did no doubt suffer in the early nineteenth century from a degree of dislike and prejudice, but the principal obstacle to their political advancement was the rule that made it impossible for them to take the parliamentary oath of allegiance 'on the true faith of a Christian', and Disraeli, far from suffering this disability had been baptised as a Christian at the age of thirteen, and was a communicant member of the Church of England. He may have been a rather odd sort of Christian, but he was one all the same.

The more I studied his early career, the more obvious it appeared that 'the storm of hate and prejudice' which he had to overcome was primarily of his own making. He behaved as a young man in a way which can only be described as outrageous. He was arrogant, flamboyant, over-dressed, wildly extravagant, highly affected and apparently quite devoid of principle. He conducted with the maximum of publicity a stormy affair with the wife of a baronet and was widely believed to share her favours with the Tory ex-Lord Chancellor, Lord Lyndhurst, to whom he acted as a sort of political private secretary and general factotum. The 1830s, when all this occurred, were not as respectable as the high noon of the Victorian

era thirty or forty years later. Nevertheless, even then the spirit of
Evangelicalism was beginning to change the tone of public life, and
a debt-ridden adventurer, a dandy-cum-roué, was likely to meet a
good deal of opposition that did not simply stem from prejudice
against his racial origins. There would be just as much opposition
today. Indeed, I often wonder whether a modern 'young Disraeli'
would ever have got the nomination to a Tory seat at all, let alone a
fairly safe one which Disraeli obtained in 1837.

Then there was the matter of Disraeli's political consistency and
far-sightedness. It is quite true that as a young man he held some
original views on the nature of true Toryism, which are adumbrated
in his novels *Coningsby*, *Sybil* and *Tancred* – the concept of 'Young
England'. But it is very doubtful whether it was that ideology which
prompted him to attack Peel. I wonder whether we would have
heard of any of this if Disraeli had been given the minor office which
he asked of Peel in 1841 (and which in 1846 he denied asking). Peel
quite reasonably declined – Disraeli had no real claim – and thus
made an enemy for life. It was only after this episode that Disraeli
begins to oppose a sort of philosophical historic Toryism to the
allegedly dry, dull pragmatism of Peel. And when Peel, in
pursuance of this pragmatism, repealed the Corn Laws which the
Party was pledged to preserve, Disraeli seized his chance. It was not
policy, but revenge. It was not even a clear-sighted way of pursuing
his own advancement, though as events turned out, it led to the
leadership of the House of Commons.

As for the story that Disraeli educated his party into the realities of
the modern world and that his Reform Bill of 1867 was a step
towards Tory democracy, much of this, too, dissolves when tested.
For one thing the initiative came from Lord Derby, not Disraeli. For
another, it soon becomes clear if one analyses the day-to-day course
of events in the House of Commons, that the Conservative Reform
Bill, introduced after the Liberals had failed to pass a similar measure
and resigned, was essentially a tactical manoeuvre – a means of
keeping their opponents, who were in a nominal majority, divided
and themselves in office; not a far-sighted measure to enfranchise
the 'Tory working man'. Indeed, Disraeli *accepted* great increases in
the franchise forced on him by the Liberals, but he did not *initiate*
them, whatever he may have said afterwards. The policy was not
the implementation of a young man's ideals; it was rather one of
enlightened expediency. Of course it was none the worse for that
and there is a lot to be said for enlightened expediency. But the fact

alters whether for good or ill one's picture of Disraeli.

And the same is true of his great premiership from 1874 to 1880. What do we associate with that? For generations the orthodox answer has been social reform, empire and strong foreign policy. Like all stereotypes, it is partly correct. Indeed it would not otherwise have become a stereotype at all. But a closer look reveals a rather different picture. A strong foreign policy survives. This really was Disraeli's great interest. He believed that he inherited the mantle of Palmerston, and he regarded Gladstone's conciliatory internationalism with contempt. But Disraeli *talked* about empire rather than *acted*, and the two expansionist wars of his day in Afghanistan and Zululand occurred despite him, not because of him. As for social reform, a whole bundle of important measures went through in 1875–6, but they owed little to him, and when he got into office in February 1874, the whole of the first session was occupied by the Archbishop of Canterbury's measure about ecclesiastic ritual and clergymen's dress – largely because Disraeli simply had not thought of a governmental programme.

But the problem of interpreting a man's mature career is perhaps less difficult than that of assessing the driving force behind him. Biographies are, after all, about men and women of achievement, and one of the great questions is what it was that gave them the sense of duty, ambition and determination to become people of achievement. The late Sir William (later Lord) Beveridge left a diary note in his earlier years as Director of the London School of Economics to the effect that it was his ambition 'to write the life of the statistically average man'. Fortunately he never embarked on this dismal project. Anything more boring it would be hard to conceive. Biographers are sometimes accused of being snobs. If the word is used, not in the sense of obsequiousness to dukes, but in the sense of being interested in people who have risen high in the world of art, science, business, learning, law or politics, who have *done* something, who have counted in public esteem either in their own time or posthumously, then the biographer should plead guilty and accept the charge as a compliment. The social historian is concerned with the 'common man'. The biographer is not.

But the intriguing problem remains. What is that constitutes the uncommon man? Where does he get his motivating force? What in Jeremy Bentham's words are his 'springs of action'? The question has only to be asked to be susceptible of almost as many different replies as there are uncommon men. Although there is no simple comprehensive answer, there is one area in which most of us instinctively feel we should look. 'The child is father to the man' may not be a universally valid dictum, but there is enough evidence suggesting the long and profound effects of childhood experiences to make every serious biographer wish to know a great deal about his subject's early years which may or may not be his formative years as well. Dickens's experience at a blacking factory, Byron's treatment by his nurse, the Kaiser's withered arm, are clear examples, but there are many less obvious and more subtle.

The difficulty is that the records of famous figures very rarely extend back into their childish or adolescent years. A few doting parents may sometimes preserve stories or letters, but what children reveal to their parents is a very small part of the truth, and those who observe them from a non-parental standpoint have no cause to record or even remember. After all how is one even to guess that this or that little boy or little girl, or even this or that teenager is' one day going to stride on the stage of the nation or the world.

There is one notable exception: the children of royalty. With the heirs to thrones – indeed even with the remoter relatives who might come into the line of succession – there is a guarantee of prominence or at least a sporting chance of prominence. The behaviour or royal children is naturally more closely noticed, and their illnesses and characteristics recorded. To take one example: the symptoms of the hereditary disease, porphyria, which is now said to be the cause of George III's 'madness'. It is probably only in a reigning family that these would have been recorded over so many generations, thus making it possible for medical historians to construct what – at least to the layman – seems a plausible diagnosis. Likewise with personal qualities. We know far more about the young Queen Victoria than we do about any contemporary of hers at that age.

Because children write few letters and because the letters of fifteen and sixteen-year olds or even beyond that are seldom preserved, we have little documentary evidence to go on. Autobiographies can help and the young sometimes keep diaries, but how often do diaries survive, and how far can autobiographies be trusted? This is the great biographical gap. One can argue how much it really matters. If it does matter, then very few perfect biographies can every be written.

I was fascinated with this problem over Disraeli. There can be no doubt that more than most figures who rise to the top he was driven on by a compulsive ambition, a determination to *be* someone. In this respect he differed from other statesmen no less ruthless and determined than himself. Joseph Chamberlain and Lloyd George hated each other, but they had one thing in common; they wanted to achieve particular objectives, they wanted by legislation or administration to change and improve the standards of life at home, and in Chamberlain's case to reconstitute the whole structure of the British Empire, although this was something which he never managed in the end to do. But he wanted to do it. As for Lloyd George, he left a lasting imprint on the social and economic order and he gave a notable impetus to the war effort in 1917–18. Both of them were quite genuinely ready to take second place if their objectives could be thus obtained. Joseph Chamberlain never did become Prime Minister. Lloyd George would have been quite happy to direct the war effort under Asquith's suzerainty if Asquith would agree – which he did not, thus forcing Lloyd George to take the first place.

Disraeli was less concerned with doing things than being someone. Of course the dichotomy is not complete. You cannot be Prime Minister without doing something, and I am not suggesting that Disraeli once in office did not have policies and purposes, some of which he pushed through with great vigour against the wishes of his entire cabinet. His conduct of foreign affairs in the eastern crisis of 1876–78 is an object lesson to anyone who believes that prime ministerial power first came into being in a big way under Lloyd George. But the basic truth remains that Disraeli wanted above all to get to the top and that he had no particular ideas about what to do before he got there. So the question of his 'springs of action', of the forces that drove him onwards and upwards is particularly interesting.

I found certain clues which I believe point to the cause, though I cannot be sure. First and most obviously plausible is his racial origin. With a foreign name, dark curls, pallid complexion and prominent nose, he was obviously different from English boys, and the difference was not likely to be unnoticed in an age when schoolboys were more intolerant and prejudiced than they are today. There are allusions in Disraeli's novels to the hero's schooldays, suggesting friendships broken or rebuffed, great fights in which the hero triumphs. Disraeli could be very artificial in his novels, but these passages have the authentic ring of personal experience, and the pattern of the boy of brilliance and genius sneered at by the common herd and determined to show them what he could do is repeated too often to be a mere adventitious piece of novelistic imagination. Disraeli felt himself to be an outsider. If he could not 'belong', at least he could rule.

The other clue is a remark by his sister, Sarah, when they were both in their forties and their parents were dead. Disraeli wrote a memoir, very inaccurate, of his father and family as the preface to a new edition of Isaac D'Israeli's published works. Reading it Sarah was at once struck by a curious omission. 'I do wish', she wrote to her brother, 'that one felicitous stroke, one tender word had brought our dear Mother into the picture.' If Disraeli replied – and like most of us he tended not to answer inconvenient questions – his reply has not survived.

This remark of Sarah Disraeli suddenly made other things fall into place, some negative, some positive. Disraeli left a quantity of autobiographical memoranda, but his mother is never mentioned. In her last year Disraeli, well on the way to the leadership of the party, made a brilliant speech in 1847. 'Mama at last confesses', wrote Sarah to Disraeli's wife, 'that she never before thought Dis was equal to Mr Pitt. So you see it pleases all variety of hearers or reader.' It was too late. She died a month later, and her real verdict had been delivered many years before when she wrote, admittedly in defence of her son, a letter to John Murray, the great publisher, who had quarrelled with Benjamin, then a young man of twenty-one. Murray had good cause to think that Disraeli had treated him badly. Maria D'Israeli, however, came to the rescue, reproaching Murray for claiming to have been

> deceived by the plans of a boy of twenty whom you had known from his cradle and whose resources you must have as well known as his father and had you condescended to consult that father the folly might not have been committed.
>
> You might then, Sir, perhaps would have found, tho' a clever boy, he was no 'prodigy'.

Whether Disraeli ever saw the letter we do not know. Probably not. But the attitude he must have known, and he could never accept it. He was in his own eyes something much more than 'a clever boy'. Indeed he was quite right. He *was* a 'prodigy', a genius in many ways. All his life, with his mistresses, his wife, his sister and those elderly objects of his widowerhood infatuation, Lady Chesterfield and Lady Bradford, Disraeli is looking for a mother-figure. Lady

Sykes, object of his grand amour in the 1830s, refers to him as 'my child' and signs 'your mother'. Is it fanciful to see one of the springs of action of Disraeli's youth as a sense of not being appreciated by a mother whom he would have loved to love, of resentment at being treated on a par with his sister and his two rather mediocre brothers, with the corresponding reaction in a determination to show her that he *was* a 'prodigy' and not just a clever boy? These things are not susceptible of final proof. Biography is not an exact science, or indeed a science at all. It may be that alienation from his schoolfellows (significantly he had very few friends of his own age at any time in his life) was not as important as I have suggested. It may be that I am reading too much into his relations with his mother. This explanation of his ambitiousness may be wrong, but an explanation is needed, and it has to be sought in his case somewhere in his youth. I quote the whole case as one example of a perennial biographical problem – one of the least easy to solve, yet one to which the biographer must at least try to find a solution, however hard it may be.

I have spoken at some length about Disraeli because the problems there are ones of which I have had first-hand knowledge. I have mentioned the problem of interpretation because that is the first and greatest problem of biography and it arose in a particularly acute form there. But if interpretation is one major consideration in the art of biography, presentation is the other. How does one put across the picture which rightly or wrongly one has decided to be the correct one?

The first necessity is, of course, the ability to write good English. By this I do not mean that the biographer needs to be a Macaulay, a Gibbon, let alone a Carlyle. But no biography is worth reading unless it is written clearly and unambiguously, unless the sentences flow easily and unless one can read on without continuously having to look back to find out to whom the pronouns refer and what the sentence actually means. Moreover, the biographer must possess the sense of paragraphs. Nothing is worse on the one hand than great monolithic paragraphs which cover a whole page or more, or on the other a series of staccato divisions which make the page look like a leader in the *Sun*.

These qualities ought to be taken for granted. It is a measure of the deterioration of English writing that one cannot do so today in the way that one could fifty or a hundred years ago. More difficult are the wider questions of how to arrange the book, how to emphasise both the crises and the passing years, when to quote and at what length, what to put in and what to leave out.

The Victorians tended to put in everything (except sex of course), and to quote at great length. But they wrote in general with the conscious intention of depicting the hero, the man who was in some way admirable. No doubt defects (again excluding sex) would be mentioned, but the general purpose of the Victorian and of much of post-Victorian biography was to show the good man with a purpose overcoming the obstacles of the outside world. It is perhaps one of the improvements in attitude today that we are readier to recognise the non-heroic nature of most men, readier to see that people are on the whole their own worst enemies, that their difficulties and frustrations come more often from within than without.

The desire to show the hero was combined with a profound belief in the value of the written word. The Victorians were great exponents of massive documentation. Here in a sense they were modelling themselves on Boswell who does indeed print many a letter to or from Johnson verbatim. But they failed to see that Boswell's genius lay precisely in the assimilation of documents and personal recollections of a biographer with astonishing percipience and an extraordinary memory. Scarcely any Victorian biographers and very few since have had the opportunity thus to record the sayings, foibles, gestures of the person about whom they wrote. When they did they seldom took the opportunity.

Morley's *Life of Gladstone* (3 volumes, 1903), for example, might in other hands have been a Boswell's Johnson. Morley knew Gladstone in his later years very well indeed and was personally involved in some of his most critical political decisions, but a curious veil of reticence comes down. Or rather, perhaps, it is that Morley could not discard his Liberal spectacles. To him Gladstone was a man who beginning as a Tory, gradually discarded obscurantist principles, and developed into the great broad-minded adherent of liberty and the Liberal Party. In fact Gladstone was a much more complicated figure than this, and Morley quotes, though without alluding to their significance, many remarks of the Grand Old Man which substantiate a different view. It is to Morley's credit, as it was to Froude on Henry VIII, that he does not suppress, and that he leaves the reader with evidence to draw a very divergent conclusion from his own. But because he does not face the reality of Gladstone's subtle and convoluted character, his profound sense of guilt, his desire for self-mortification, his extraordinary conservatism with a small 'c', he fails to reach the top level. His life of Gladstone is a good biography, but it is not a great one.

The problem of presentation is in a large measure one of quotation. The art of how much and what to quote fom the subject's correspondence is one of the most difficult tasks of the biographer. If one quotes too much one can easily fall into the error which I mentioned earlier of thinking that the documents speak for themselves, and tell their own story. One of the highly praised biographies of our time, still incomplete, seems to me to verge upon this error. I refer to the multi-volume life of Winston Churchill begun by the late Randolph Churchill and continued by Martin Gilbert. Randolph Churchill set out with the purpose of telling the story as far as possible in his father's words. On the title page of both his volumes he quotes Lockhart's avowed aim in his life of Sir Walter Scott: 'He shall be his own biographer.' Martin Gilbert, though omitting the quotation, has also chosen to narrate the life largely in Churchill's words – and Churchill was a prolific and brilliant writer – with the result that quotation tends to swamp judgement. The biographer is almost too modest. One wants him to stand back from his subject more often and to say what *he* thinks, how *he* judges Churchill's actions, and also how other people judged them. I am not saying that Martin Gilbert never does this at all. I am simply saying that he does not do it enough – anyway for one reader's taste – and that a biographer must be something more than an editor, however scholarly, of documents and letters.

The temptation to over-quote arises particularly when the subject of biography is an articulate and entertaining writer. I had no temptation to do this with an earlier biography which I wrote, that of Andrew Bonar Law (1955), whose many virtues did not include the slightest flicker of literary grace. Indeed he was about as dull a letter-writer as one could encounter among Prime Ministers, the late Lord Attlee being a runner-up. On the other hand, Disraeli, like Byron, was incapable of writing a dull word and his style is wholly idiosyncratic. Even his replies to dinner invitations bear a personal imprint which is not quite like that of anyone else. It is, therefore, an easy way out, when inspiration flags and the mental lamp burns low, to fill in with extracts from the most quotable of all great men – an easy way out, but wrong. The danger of overdoing it is the danger into which Monypenny and Buckle to some degree fell – the danger of seeing the whole political scene through their hero's eyes.

And this raises another central problem of presentation. How far does the biographer tell the story as if he was in the shoes of his hero, or at any rate as if he was his contemporary? How far does he use the historian's advantage of hindsight? Clearly he must to some extent. The whole point of history (of which biography is a subsection) is that we do know what happened in the end and that we can exercise a synoptic view of a man's career which neither he nor any contemporary could do. Knowing that Disraeli did become Prime Minister in the end, we can try to assess how he did so, decide whether it was the result of luck or deliberate planning, and consider how far, when he did reach the top, his own cry was true – 'Power! It has come to me too late. There were days when on waking I felt I could move dynasties and governments; but that has passed away.'

Yet the biographer has to remember all the while that the future is concealed from the eyes of the man he is writing about. It is worth his while now and then to consider how his hero would have appeared to history if he had been cut off – not in his youth, of course, but at an age when people often do die. Winston Churchill was on the verge of sixty-five when the Second World War broke out. Had he died in 1939, he would have gone down to history as 'a splendid failure'. There is indeed a study of his career from 1900 to 1939 by Robert Rhodes James, entitled *Churchill, a Study in Failure* (1970), and it is well worth reading.

If Disraeli had retired from politics as he seriously considered at about the same age in the middle sixties, he would only have been remembered as an eccentric novelist who somehow got as high as being Chancellor of the Exchequer. If Gladstone had done what he said he was going to do in 1874, retire at the age of sixty-five, because he 'deeply desired an interval between parliament and the grave', how differently we would look at him! His would indeed have been a career of success, but all the drama, the tragedy, the excitement was still to come – Prime Minister thrice more, the Midlothian campaign, Ireland, Parnell – all these strange and exciting episodes lay in the future, with the last chapter of all, the indomitable daemonic figure taking office for the fourth time at the age of eighty-two, piloting through the House of Commons single-handed the most controversial Bill of the century – the second Home Rule Bill – only to see it crash to defeat in the House of Lords. And we would not have had my favourite scene in modern political history. When at last in 1894 the Grand Old Man announced his resignation many of the Cabinet were in tears. Sir William Harcourt drew out of his pocket a piece of paper with notes for a farewell encomium, which, as Lord Rosebery observed, was yellow with age. Gladstone listened cold and unmoved. 'Resigned!', he said afterwards to a friend, 'I was kicked out.' And he referred to the last meeting of his colleagues as 'that blubbering cabinet'.

The point is that the biographer must, of course, make use of all the advantages of hindsight. That is what he is there for. But he must never forget that to his subject and his subject's contemporaries their future was as much a mystery and a blank as our future is to us. He must never write as if there was a pre-ordained fate for his hero, and never try to explain his actions as if they were steps towards the fulfilment of a manifest destiny.

Perhaps the greatest problem of the biographer – and it is partly one of interpretation, partly of presentation – is that of perspective. It arises in two ways. There is the problem of detaching the life from the times. How much of the 'times' is one to take for granted as far as the reader is concerned? How much of the background needs to be sketched in? It partly depends on the place and the period, and, of course, the readers for whom one is writing. I am a strong believer in the view that biographies should be written for the intelligent, but not necessarily historically expert, reader. It is necessary to give more general background to an English reader if one is writing a life of Louis Napoleon or Bismarck than if one is writing about Gladstone or Disraeli of Stanley Baldwin or Lloyd George. The problem is more daunting if one goes further back in time, for the background of the life of say St Jerome, to name one very successful biography by John Kelly (1975), who has achieved this balance admirably. It is perhaps a point to mention that political biographies must be of a certain length if they are to be more than character sketches. There has been a spate of short biographies of about 60–70 000 words recently. I have some doubts about this genre. I suspect that something like Johnson's *Lives of the Poets*, let us say So and So's *Lives of the Prime Ministers* (selected individuals) might be worth doing, but one would expect them to be brief pen portraits of 25–30 000 words at the most – somewhat like Winston Churchill's *Great Contemporaries* (1937). Otherwise I believe that a serious single life must be longer than 60–70 000 words to be effective. It is not possible to explain the complications of the political background against which a Prime Minister operates in a book of less than nearly double that length. Political history which is the background of political biography cannot be condensed beyond a certain point without becoming positively misleading.

That is one aspect of perspective. The other aspect is the distance of time from which one is surveying one's subject. And here we come to an important division of biographical categories. There is one category, naturally a minority of all the biographies ever written, which can be described as the 'first biography' or 'the official biograhy'. By this I mean the first life to be written after someone's death by an author with full access to the person's private and political or literary papers. Then there are in effect all the others which are written subsequently and at varying intervals of time.

The first category has peculiar advantages and also great disadvantages. I have experienced both categories. My life of Bonar Law was in the first, though it came out over thirty years after his death, and my life of Disraeli was in the second. The great advantage of the first is that one can consult people who knew the person concerned. One may indeed – though not in my case – have known him personally. Of course there are difficulties here, but the mere fact of having heard someone talk, seen his gestures, known his mannerisms, is an asset. Even to have talked to other people who did is an asset. Disraeli died just long enough ago for that to be impossible. At its best the official or first biography can be a great work – indeed, if not 'definitive' (and what is ever 'definitive'), at any rate something on which all others depend. Froude's life of Carlyle written within a few years of Carlyle's death is one of the great biographies of the English language.

But there are problems and I certainly found myself involved in some of them.

> I should shrink with horror [wrote Gibbon] from the modern history of England, where every character is a problem, and every reader a friend or an enemy; where a writer is supposed to hoist a flag of party, and is devoted to damnation by the adverse faction.

The battles between Conservative and Liberals and between rival factions within the Liberals, which had raged during and after the First World War, were very far from dead when I wrote well over thirty years later. The curious who look at the correspondence columns of *The Times* early in 1956 will find no less than 108 column inches devoted to the important question whether or not Bonar Law when he visited Asquith's country house in Oxfordshire on Whit Monday 1916 found the Prime Minister playing bridge with three ladies. Moreover – and though this was not a biography, the principle is the same – a similar row broke out in 1952 when I published my edition of *Haig's Diaries* with a biographical introduction. It was the first occasion on which Haig's very adverse view of the French Army was revealed. The late Lord Norwich (Duff Cooper) who lived in Paris was asked to resign from the Traveller's Club simply because he had reviewed the book favourably in the *Continental Daily Mail*.

Duff Cooper's role raised indeed an important question about 'first' biographies. What can you legitimately insert or omit at that stage? He was Haig's 'official biographer' in the mid-1930s, but he was also a member of the Cabinet, strongly pro-French and anti-German. He told me quite frankly that he deliberately left out Haig's views on the French for political reasons; and one can see how awkward it would have been for a cabinet minister to put them in. But, of course, an important element in Haig's motivation for some of his most criticised offensives was thus omitted.

To take another example, Sir Roy Harrod writing his life of Keynes five years after Keynes's death deliberately omitted all reference to the homosexual side of Keynes and the whole Bloomsbury Set to which Keynes belonged. At that time (1950) no doubt these things were less discussed than today, but even then they were mentionable. Sir Roy did so because he thought that the resultant prejudice created might damage the efficacy of Keynes's economic policies which he regarded as even more vital posthumously to the salvation of the country than in Keynes's life time.

Then there are other self-imposed reticences. Froude's *Carlyle* is a great book and it deals at length with his unhappy quarrel-torn marriage, but Froude never hints what we now know that he well knew – namely that Carlyle was impotent. On any view this was a highly relevant consideration for a biographer. Victorian usage perhaps did make such a matter unmentionable, but it meant that a very important factor in Thomas and Jane Welsh Carlyle's stormy and tragic life was omitted entirely. To take another omission, it was well known that T. E. Lawrence 'of Arabia' was illegitimate; and – much more important than the fact of illegitimacy – his whole life was tormented by the knowledge. Many books on him appeared, but when Richard Aldington wrote the first which revealed the truth about his birth there was an uproar. Yet it is clearly impossible fully to understand what made Lawrence the man he was without some knowledge of these circumstances.

The biographer who writes at a longer interval of time does not have these inhibitions. There is no longer a family to be offended – anyway not much offended, for when once those who actually knew the person are dead, the biographer can write more freely. There are no longer friends with a vested interest of loyalty, affection or gratitude who spring to the defence against every charge. There is in one sense likely to be more information available. Fresh sets of documents become open for inspection and, although the 'official biographer' will have had access to the subject's own correspondence in and out, he is not so likely to have access to the letters of other people who wrote to each other about the subject of the biography – often one of the most valuable and enlightening source of all.

Above all he has the advantage of that longer perspective in which he can set the 'life' amidst the 'times' and perhaps see more clearly than any contemporary or near contemporary what the meaning of the 'times' was. But, of course, he misses the freshness and the immediacy. How fascinating, I often thought, to have heard Disraeli speak or even to have been able to ask questions from those who had heard him speak. But he was just out of reach of even second-hand evidence of that sort – so near and yet so far.

I have surveyed biography in a somewhat haphazard and higgledy-piggledy way, but then it is a rather shapeless subject, hard to define or regulate. I will end by a brief word on the mechanics of biography, and I will simply say that, however fascinating it may be, it is very hard work. It is far easier to chair committee meetings, send a memorandum to one's colleagues, bargain over some deal, make a speech or appear on television than it is to write a serious book.

One must do a lot of research, and research can be wearisome. Yet it is important not to do too much research. Those who compile endless card indexes, who perpetually put off the task of actually writing in the hope that yet another document or cache of papers will throw a flood of light on the scene are liable never to set pen to paper at all. A certain moment comes when one should write. I began my book on Bonar Law in the middle and wrote an account of the way in which he actually became so unexpectedly leader of the Conservative Party. Of course I had to rewrite most of it at least once, but the point was that I had enough to go on for a draft and the very process of writing stimulated my interest again.

It is important to bear in mind that in historical research as in other things there is a law of diminishing returns, that a moment comes when commonsense or one's 'hunch' tells one that, however much you go on you will not really do more than dot 'i's and cross 't's. There is now a great project instituted in Canada to microfilm and eventually publish *all* Disraeli's letters. Those concerned have been far more assiduous than I was. They have discovered masses of letters of whose existence I did not know. I wish I had, especially the letters which, I am told, reveal that in order to avoid being arrested for debt before he took the parliamentary oath in 1837 Disraeli was smuggled into the House disguised as a pastry cook. Yet, although that episode would have made an enjoyable paragraph or two in my book, it would not have altered my basic view of Disraeli. Contretemps of the sort were a regular feature of his early days. This one merely crosses a 't'. It is not very likely that the great compilation will fundamentally change one's picture of Disraeli, though it may well throw light on other by-ways of Victorian history.

The truth is that works of biography and history are always imperfect. One can never get all the evidence, and if one tries to do so, one will never finish the book, perhaps not even set pen to paper. Life is finite and limited for the biographer as well as his subject.

Perhaps I should end appropriately with a quotation from one of Dr Johnson's *Lives of the Poets* – in this case Alexander Pope, who had taken five years instead of the promised two to translate the *Iliad*:

> According to this calculation, the progress of Pope may seem to have been slow; but the distance is commonly very great between actual performance and speculative possibility. It is natural to suppose that as much as has been done today may be done tomorrow; but on the morrow some difficulty emerges, or some external impediment obstructs. Indolence, interruption, business, and pleasure, all take their turns of retardation; and every long work is lengthened by a thousand causes that can and ten thousand that cannot, be recounted. Perhaps no extensive and multifarious performance was ever effected within the term originally fixed in the undertaker's mind. He that runs against Time has an antagonist not subject to casualties.

7

How I Fell into Biography
Michael Holroyd

The writer under whose influence I first became a biographer was Hugh Kingsmill. Kingsmill believed that the value of a biography could be increased by an autobiographical preface that helped the reader to find his or her own particular truth within a book. So in that spirit I will preface my own contribution with some autobiographical observations, applying my own techniques to myself while attempting to describe how I fell into biography.

To begin at the beginning – as most biographers do (they are the slaves of chronology): I was born on 27 August 1935 according to my mother and on 29 August 1935 in the opinion of my father. An initial difficulty here. For this was one of the many matters about which my parents did not agree. Later this year (1985) I shall be celebrating my fiftieth birthday twice – once, scrupulously, for each parent. Yet the ownership of two birthdays is perfectly proper for a biographer who must continually lead two separate but overlapping lives – his own and that of the person about whom he is currently writing. It is an aging process.

My parents met – as parents sometimes do – in the middle of the North Sea. The moon was shining and while they remained all at sea they got on famously well. But eventually they struck land, the marriage went on the rocks, and I landed up at Maidenhead with my paternal grandparents, one faintly Scottish the other largely Irish. Since my mother, who was Swedish, married a Hungarian gentleman and my father married a French lady, my background can be made to sound excitingly polyglot and cosmopolitan. Yet for all that, Maidenhead does not sound a very exciting hole: nor was it. While there I was a great worry to my grandparents. They did not know what to do with 'the boy' as I was called. Sometimes they generously asked me for ideas as to how I should occupy my days, and years. But I gave no help. I could think of little but filling my head upstairs in my bedroom with book-adventures.

My grandparents knew nothing about literature, but that did not prevent them thinking very highly of it. It was my grandfather's opinion that literature had flourished in the age of Shakespeare and come to an end with Dickens, Thackeray and Trollope. My grandmother, being his wife, agreed. When I told my family that I intended to write, and worse still, that I wanted to write biography (which to my grandfather's mind had begun and ended with Boswell – and my grandmother agreed) there was a good deal of consternation. For a time they wondered whether to call in some sort of medical person. It was obvious to them that I should be a structural engineer, or plasma physicist, or biochemist, or perhaps radiologist – they weren't absolutely certain which. They simply felt that I ought to join the scientific age that was developing in the twentieth century. That was where the jobs were: that was where the money was. There was nothing whatever wrong in this reasoning – except perhaps for the fact that I had no scientific or mathematical abilities. I argued so obstinately amid a cacophony of French, Hungarian, Irish and Swedish voices that eventually it was suggested I enter the law. Finally my country came to the rescue in the shape of two years' National Service – after which, it appeared to many, I was good for practically nothing. But in any case, as it now seems to me, education is not exclusively a matter of jobs. It may increasingly be concerned with how we learn to live without jobs or with part-time jobs: how, in short, we can convert the unemployed into the self-employed – in which case literature and the arts may be seen as having primary importance in a microchip society after all.

While other people went up to university, I went and read literature at the Maidenhead Public Library. I commanded there a magnificent range of books, from ancient classics to the latest publications, and was provided with excellent lighting, heating, the service of trained librarians, the most up-to-date magazines. I lived like a king at the Maidenhead Public Library. This caused some bewilderment at home and eventually my aunt was sent to investigate. She found the place much better than she feared, and soon joined it, though she insisted on grilling the books she borrowed in a medium oven to exterminate the germs. And what my aunt did others were doing. Private libraries were closing down and a whole new section of society was cautiously beginning to share in the common cultural wealth of the country. You could tell the most popular titles in those days, not by Public Lending Right statistics as now, but by the residual heat from middle-class Aga stoves.

It was in this library that I had come by chance across the books of Hugh Kingsmill. Kingsmill gave me exactly what I wanted in my late teens and early twenties. No professor had chosen him for me: I had found him for myself. What he gave me was not part of the schoolroom but what goes on outside it – what is enjoyed rather than endured. What was it that appealed to me about Kingsmill? First of all, I think, he made literature real to me – that is to say, he made the connection factually and imaginatively between what we read and how we live. Secondly, he was an isolated figure, as I felt myself to be. He belonged to no fashionable school of writing, neither inhabiting Bloomsbury nor contributing to *Scrutiny*. He did not paddle in literary politics: I felt he had a deeper focus. His judgements, delivered with wit and epigrammatic flair, were moralistically intuitive to an extraordinary degree. He did not categorise writers simply by their politics or sex. He saw the world as being inhabited by two species of human being: those who were motivated by the will, and those inspired by the imagination. Men and women of will imposed order through force; men and women of imagination detected an order and a harmony underlying the discord of our lives. At the present stage of evolution, Kingsmill suggested, people of will tended to rise in society to positions of executive power and to confront people of will in other groups or countries. This was why, in our history, so many warring factions, however bitterly opposed, tended to resemble each other. That was why there were wars that large numbers of imaginative individuals on both sides did not want. Of course this is a very simple approximation and paraphrase of Kingsmill's ideas. In most people the contradictory impulses of will and imagination co-exist, and we are constantly at war against our worst selves, constantly tempted to externalise the enemy within. This co-existence and conflict was the theme of much of Kingsmill's biographical writing as well as his fiction. One of the reasons why his ideas attracted me was that they enabled me to attribute my idleness, day-dreaming, love of music, my apprehension of the competitive spirit, to superior imaginative qualities.

There was one further reason, I think, why Kingsmill appealed to me. His own life, in so far as I could find out anything about it, was utterly different from my own and my family's. That was a great recommendation. I had taken up reading so that I could travel in my mind and emotions while remaining stationary in my bedroom and in the public library at Maidenhead. I took up biography after reading Kingsmill so that I might enter the lives of people whom I had chosen rather than found myself with. Therefore I have not chosen subjects who resembled me – that would defeat the purpose. I set out to escape into my subjects' lives rather than identify myself with them. I am, I can reveal, unbearded despite writing biographies of Lytton Strachey (1967–8), Augustus John (1974–5) and currently Bernard Shaw. This is a great surprise to officials meeting me at railway stations. To them I try to explain that I explore the lives and characters of my biographees as a traveller explores foreign countries, and that I come back from these explorations with a language learnt, something new that I have seen, felt, experienced, assimilated – and can pass on to my readers. It is a learning process and a teaching process simultaneously. A good biographical subject, it seems to me, is simply one that stirs much feeling and provokes much thought and may therefore call the best writing out of the biographer for the reader. Under such circumstances, at a different level, a two-fold process of discovery takes place. As he pursues his research and finds out more about his subject, the biographer makes discoveries about himself. Features below the conscious level of his personality emerge, and what they are will depend upon the forces released by the meeting of two lives. This is a natural evolution in the making of a book. You cannot choose your subject too carefully: but you cannot predict what will happen.

My first subject was Kingsmill himself. I have to report that after the appearance of my book (in 1964) he remained as stubbornly unknown to the general reading public as he had been before it. Perhaps that was predictable. However, I count it as something of a diplomatic triumph to have persuaded a publisher to bring out a biography of a neglected author by an unknown writer. My next subject was not unknown, but out of fashion: Lytton Strachey. In choosing him I began to set a pattern for my future work – that of promoting a minor character in my previous book to be the subject of my next book. Kingsmill had been charged, in so far as he wrote biographies himself, with being 'School of Strachey'. To deal with this allegation I studied Strachey's books and grew increasingly interested in them – to the extent of going on to write his life. A minor but important figure in that book was Augustus John who had offered Strachey at a crucial moment in his career an alternative lifestyle – that of British Bohemia with its headquarters in Chelsea in place of the intellectual areas of Cambridge and Bloomsbury. And Augustus John's portraits of Bernard Shaw were to some extent trigger movements that shot G. B. S. into range as my present biographical victim. All three lived in the same hundred-years-or-so span, though they led very different lives within that span. In the Bloomsbury, Fabian and the Bohemian cultures that they represent I have tried to weave a texture of the period. To write about any other period I would have to send myself back to school, and as I have explained I am too old for that. Besides, it is difficult when travelling back further than the nineteenth century to pick up that tone of intimacy that I find essential for biography.

Since I make my living from what I write I count as a professional biographer, though I feel myself in some respects to be an amateur. Amateurishness is a well-known English trait. At its worst it produces the sort of pallid impressionism that Bernard Crick trenchantly attacked in his biography of George Orwell. It does, however, avoid the arid professionalism that has little *raison d'être* other than the lengthening of an academic curriculum vitae and the securing of tenure. For my part I write, with much complaining, for the love of the thing – which is not to say that it necessarily runs smoothly.

I have no General Theory of Biography: I do have general reflections. As a branch of literature biography is still comparatively young. It began as praise, and was developed as a method of conferring historical endorsement on the lives of rulers and saints, instilling in its readers a spirit of admiration and the habit of imitation. As part of the machinery for preserving the status quo, biography came to resemble a shapeless petrified jelly inside which some wobbling human remains were vaguely visible: a life in aspic.

It was with Samuel Johnson that biography entered the modern age. He declared that the first business of the biographer was not necessarily to dwell on 'those performances and incidents which produce vulgar greatness', but to 'lead the thoughts into domestic privacies, and to display the minute details of daily life'. Though devoted to piety, Johnson was preoccupied with human nature. It was fitting that Boswell, leaving the piety aside, should have shared this preoccupation and brought Johnson so wonderfully back to life for us – especially whenever he himself appears on the page. For Boswell was a great diary writer, making the connection between biographers and journalists.

Then came earnestness. Biography was crucially infected by the blight of Victorianism which concealed private life under a prim camouflage and pumped the national energy into vulgar imperialism. Biography reflected this public vulgarity and private prudery until it began to be rescued by Edmund Gosse's *Father and Son* (1907) and then, more spectacularly, Lytton Strachey's *Eminent Victorians* (1918). Since then the boundaries have been enlarged and, with such a modern masterworks as Richard Ellmann's *James Joyce* (1959) and Victoria Glendinning's *Edith Sitwell* (1981) contain the full range of human experience. It is not only a question of the legitimacy of subject-matter, from investment of income to expenditure of sex, but also the variety of narrative modes. Biography exists as psychological melodrama in Strachey's *Elizabeth and Essex* (1928), as detective work in A. J. A. Symons's *The Quest for Corvo* (1955), as crime reconstruction in Truman Capote's *In Cold Blood* (1966), and as an experiment with time in Nigel Nicolson's *Portrait of a Marriage* (1973); as a collection of short stories in Harold Nicolson's *Some People* (1927), as physical and metaphysical travel writing in Richard Holmes's *Footsteps* (1985), and so on.

It was Richard Holmes who recently wrote that 'we have in fact witnessed something very rare: the rise to power of a new literary genre.' We all know what he means, and yet this rise is by no means universal. Biography has risen in the English speaking world but not elsewhere. When I went with a delegation of writers to Moscow in 1984, the Russians were unable to match me with any biographer of their own. Indeed I was in one sense the most 'revolutionary' member of our team and my pronouncements about the progressive role of biography in society were completely excised from the record of our conference – it was as if I had said nothing. Russian biography, I learned, had reached a stage approximately equivalent to our own in 1850. But that is also true of various dictatorships in Western Europe where it is still used as a reinforcement of the existing order and never to enquire into the future by re-examining the past and setting it in a new direction.

From Boswell to Strachey biographers have been an unrespectable crew, given atrociously to gossip and possessing the merit of bad taste – which is to say that they have not conformed to the polite fashions of their day. Even Carlyle, for all his brave opinions, had difficulties in accepting his own biographer Froude. The honest biographer, it was said, had added a new terror to death. What in fact he had done was to give the dead an opportunity of contributing to the living world. It is understandable, and right, that people should seek to protect themselves and others close to them during their lives. But if we have these necessary prevarications and sentimentalities as our only knowledge of how people lived, and as our examples of conduct, then we will mislead ourselves and make ourselves unhappy by accepting impossible standards. The lies we tell are part of the life we live and therefore part of the truth. Allowing this truth to be posthumously given, in so far as it can be recaptured and understood, may be as useful to posterity as donating kidneys and corneas. And yet it is so objectionable to think of ourselves as being dead that some of us have a fastidious repugnance to the whole process. Authors and artists have something extra to protect – the work that may live on after they have died. No wonder that writers as various as W. H. Auden, T. S. Eliot, Somerset Maugham, George Orwell and Jean Rhys have tried from beyond the grave to forbid official biographies of themselves to be written.'Biographers are generally a disease of English litera-ture', concluded George Eliot.

One of the results of this unpopularity among writers is that literary biographers have felt themselves to be outside the family of literature. That family now lives in academe. There are departments of history but no departments of biography at our universities; there are departments of English, but biography is not on the curriculum. 'Schools of literary theoreticians agree about little else except the exclusion of biography', writes Albert Camus's biographer, Patrick McCarthy. Literary biographers are divided into those who have enjoyed this excommunication because of the freedom it allows them, and those who have resented it. Among the latter, Henry James's Freudian biographer Leon Edel has become something of a hero. His *Literary Biography*, first published in 1957, argued for the centrality of biography and its value as literature – an argument that was taken up and extended in 1985 by Ira Bruce Nadel in *Biography: Fiction, Fact and Form*. 'I know of no critics in modern times', Leon Edel had protested, 'who have chosen to deal with biography as one deals with poetry or the novels.' This challenge, which inspired Professor Nadel's book, has commanded a good deal of support from American biographers themselves. The polarisation of British and American biographers is nowhere better seen than in Jeffrey Meyers's recent symposium *The Craft of Literary Biography* (1985), all the American contributors to which were professors and all but one of the British contributors freelance writers. But America often provides Britain with a glimpse into her future. Our America is here and tomorrow.

How are biographers to achieve the respectability that would crown their 'rise to power'? This unlikely question was provoked by the generous introduction at the University of East Anglia conference that Malcolm Bradbury gave me. Searching for an accurate word to describe me, he hesitated before settling on 'fantasist'. I was shocked and delighted. Shocked because instead of the violent protests I expected to see from friends and colleagues in the audience I saw smiling and nodding approval! I would remind them all that my *Augustus John* has 843 reference notes. When has fantasy ever been so underpinned? But I was delighted too because biographers long to have their inventive gifts and artistic talents recognised as much as novelists wish to have their fiction appreciated for its political and sociological content.

What Professor Bradbury was saying of course was that biography *needs* fantasy and that he hoped we would come up with some if we really wished biography to be raised to a position of power. And what he meant by fantasy is what everyone else means by the word: he meant literary criticism. In the politburo of literary criticism Professor Bradbury is plotting to make use of the ambitions of some biographers as a means of overthrowing modernist criticism (which has exiled the author and thus one of the apparent justifications of literary biography) and handing over the succession to something intellectually rigorous but more congenial. He belongs to a generation trained by Dr Leavis to overlook the author and study the text. But between the lines of text, in the blank streams of the page, lie the invisible lives of the authors, and any examination into the implications of these white areas may disturb the text in a fruitful way. For if the number of readers suggests multitudinous meanings, the author still represents a code that readers should possess for clarification of their meanings. To see only the written text and be blind to the unprinted part of the page is as restrictive to a critic as ignorance of the unconscious mind would be to a psychoanalyst.

This theory of what I call 'reconstruction' views the rewriting and reinterpretation of past lives for future generations, with all their shifts of emphasis, pattern, tone and cumulative meaning, as analogous to the oral tradition of story-telling. But before the principles of reconstruction can be established, a truce may have to be declared between those theoretical critics and working biographers who see their interests as being opposed. Recognising readers as being the repositories of meaning, the critic attaches himself as 'minder' to this democratic reader and acquires authority through

his intellectual muscle. If the author has been replaced as creator of
meaning by the team of reader-and-critic, how doubly redundant
then is the author who writes about other authors! French critics
have gone so far as to use Sartre's failure to complete his work on
Flaubert to reinforce their banishment of literary biography, and
have eliminated the entire French tradition of biography, with its
éloges of Fontenelle and Condorcet, as if it had never existed. No
wonder the biographer has been resistent to post-structuralism and
the theory of deconstruction. He opposes them for much the same
reason that poets and novelists have opposed literary biography
itself – from the fear that his magical properties will be destroyed
and his work rendered valueless. In retaliation the literary
biographer argues that the author is literally the first reader of his
text and a primary ingredient – if the notion of ownership is
objectionable – of that text. The biographer's pages may be
connected to the text they criticise, but are also independent of it and
may be treated as a special genre of fiction to which we give the
paradoxical name non-fiction.

A healthy literature needs a good cross-fertilization between
fiction and non-fiction. Many novelists use non-fiction as the raw
material of their work: many biographers feature these days in
novels – in the novels of Bernard Malamud, William Golding,
Muriel Spark, Penelope Lively and others. Biography has itself
entered that middle ground which some of the most talented
novelists have vacated, and its practitioners have learnt something
of narrative, structure and plot even from detective novels and
thrillers. Though the biographer may not invent dialogue – that is
breaking the rules of his game – he may use quotations from letters
and diaries to perform a function similar to dialogue in the narrative.
I structure my story. I say: now the reader (who is of course myself)
needs an outdoor scene at this stage – he needs a tree and a field and
the wind in his face and perhaps a spin in a car over the horizon
before I bring him back indoors and finally put him to bed. So I
manipulate the narrative to take us all where I want.

In literary biography there is the problem of how much literary
criticism to include. Sometimes it is most skilful to include none.
Since I see the life of the writer as being part of the text of his work I
tend to pick out this autobiographical sub-text. The literary
biographer, it seems to me, offers his subject the opportunity of
writing a posthumous work in collaboration, and in the mysteries of
that collaboration lie the clues to success or failure. The aim of most

biographers, who live so long with their subjects, is to establish an enduring relationship and give it literary form. Biographies create, or re-create, a world that the reader may enter, where his or her imagination may be stimulated, and some of the emotions, thoughts and laughter experienced in reading – as well as the information – may remain with the reader after the book is finished. This is a large ambition, but not so different perhaps from that of some novelists, to whom many literary biographers owe so much. Perhaps literary biography will increasingly be seen as a specialised branch of fiction – unless, that is, it comes to be categorised as a vicarious offshoot of autobiography: a fantastical twig.

8

The Biographer's Chains
Hugh Brogan

The self-confidence implicit in the use of the word 'modern' seems profoundly unsuited to conditions in the late twentieth century. The state of biography illustrates the point perfectly. There have been no really 'modern' biographies. The contrast with autobiography is painful. Throughout the century writers have vied with each other to produce autobiographies in startling new forms. Gertrude Stein's autobiography, *The Autobiography of Alice B. Toklas* (1933), is perhaps the most famous, and certainly one of the most successful, of these experiments (yet perhaps Alice B. Toklas's *Cookbook* (1954) trumped the queen); but there are dozens of them. Autobiographers have the priceless advantage that no one expects them to tell the complete, literal truth; they can stray into fiction as much as they like, and even their omissions will be read as significant. Biographers have no such licence, for it would make their enterprise pointless. The honest biographer must aim at accuracy of detail and completeness of outline (since no one could endure a biography that told everything ascertainable, and no publisher could afford to issue it – Rohan Butler's life of Choiseul (vol. I, 1980), and Martin Gilbert's endless procession of volumes about Winston Churchill, are grim illustrations of what happens when these common-sense points are ignored). A Cubist biography would be impossible, for it would too patently impose the writer's design on the subject's life, one of the worst sins a biographer can commit. Those biographers who tried to exploit psychoanalysis already look a little quaint, and their insights, much worse, unconvincing. Those psychoanalysts who tried to exploit biography have fared no better. Erikson's *Young Man Luther* (1959) is docketed as fiction; Jones's *Freud* (3 vols, 1953–57) looks dishonest. So far as I know, on one has tried to write a behaviourist biography, though it would be interesting if someone did. The endless disputes of professional historians have been of little help to biographers, for historical quarrels, of a fruitful kind, have usually been about general observations concerning the past, whereas the biographer is eternally wedded to the particular. Perhaps that is why some historians object to biography on principle. Not even individual literary talent has made much difference. Lytton Strachey's *Eminent Victorians* (1918) had many imitators, who thought it deliciously original as well as scandalous, but it is now obvious that it was in form no more (and no less) than a throwback to seventeenth and eighteenth-century techniques – to Isaac Walton and Samuel Johnson. Worse, the biographical form seems positively resistant to innovation, except of the subtlest kind. Thus, Theodore H. White's *Making of the President* (1960) – which was not even a biography – originated, so far as I know, American biographers' custom of starting their books with a prologue set in the middle of things – an innovation which has become a deadly cliché. This kind of thing:

All day the calls had come in. The successful candidate had taken some, placed some, left most to be dealt with by his weary but triumphant staff. The pleasant, shaded streets of his small home town had rapidly filled up with wellwishers and representatives of the world's press and TV networks, but the candidate had not shown himself to any of them. He had lunched quietly with his wife (cold chicken, hash browns, cole slaw, ice cream, coffee), written a little on yellow legal pads, rested. Now, at 5 p.m. Eastern Standard Time, he was making his way to the press room. At his side were his beloved Debbie and their nine children. His hero-worshipping old parents stumbled along behind. James Buchanan Wintergreen, soon to be ninety-seventh President of the United States of America, was ready for his meeting with destiny. Nervous technicians tested their hookups. All over the world conversations hushed, hearts tensed, as, adjusting his horn-rimmed bifocals (Debbie had told the *Ladies Home Journal* they made him look 'Lincolnesque') Wintergreen began to read from the notes on his yellow legal pad under the blazing television lights. He was addressing all humanity. 'My fellow Americans...'

And so on for at least ten pages more before Wintergreen is even born.

All this leads to the inevitable conclusion that the modern biographer does best to tread delicately, and that the first and last modern biography, in the sense of a work which transformed the

writer's opportunities and the reader's expectations, was Boswell's
Life of Johnson.

It is worth dwelling a little on Boswell's innovations, for they tend
to be taken for granted nowadays or, worse, misunderstood (and
then, it is always pleasant to contradict those tiresome persons, all
too common, who think that Johnson needs rescuing from his
biographer).

Boswell's interest in character was not new, nor his belief that a
great English worthy ought to be immortalised, nor his interest in
significant anecdotes. What distinguished him in the first place was
the scale on which he was prepared to work, and the years of effort,
rather the decades, that he was prepared to devote to the
achievement of his masterpiece. He steadily exploited his gifts as a
diarist, and so was able to record Johnson's conversation by the
yard. It was a specialisation forced on him, for he was in London so
seldom, and there was no other source on which he could draw to
do justice to his subject, since Johnson's letters were quite
differently expressive from his talk, and there were other collectors
of Johnsonian anecdotes and stray remarks. Not that Boswell was so
unintelligent as to neglect these or any other supplementary sources
of information. He had, if anything, a better sense of what was a
biographer's duty than had Johnson himself, if we may take as
evidence the reluctance with which Johnson (at Boswell's urging)
interviewed Lord Marchmont for the life of Pope. Boswell was
incapable of such sluggishness on a trail. He knew, also, how to
weave his materials into a single web. He knew how to write in an
unbuttoned style that brings Johnson alive as if the reader, too, were
part of the magic circle (though it is equally true that Boswell also fell
frequently into the most stilted style of his century). Above all, he
knew how to select. Everything he included was chosen to serve the
grand design. Nothing went in unless it had significance: of all his
lessons perhaps the most important. The result is a book which has
never bored anyone except those who are spontaneously averse to
the grotesque giant it depicts, or to his eccentric follower. Such
rejections of Johnson and Boswell, as if they were still living men, is
in a way as much a tribute to the biographer's art as the warmest
admiration.

The *Life of Johnson* also taught the lesson that no biography could
be final, however excellent. A biographer will make mistakes, he
will leave things out and some things he will not know. In fact his
omissions and ignorances will be sometimes as revealing as those of

an autobiographer, perhaps more so since, if the biographer is any good, they are more likely to be unconscious. The Victorians laboured to correct and supplement Boswell with footnotes. The twentieth century has tried to supersede him with new works. Neither have really made much difference to the book we read. It is still as fresh as paint, and as much an example to biographers as it ever was. When considering our craft we moderns must begin *there*.

The Victorians felt the same, but theirs was not an age in which the lessons of Boswell could really have effect. Within fifty years Tom Moore had published his *Life of Byron* (1830), and the change which had occurred became apparent. Nothing survives of Boswell's glorious indiscretion (a virtue that I might have mentioned sooner). We may honour Moore for his determined attempt to save Byron's *Memoirs* from John Murray's fireplace, and for being the first to print the poet's wonderful letters; and his book has other merits. But today its chief impression is of a pointless and unsleeping prudence. Even Boswell did not say everything he knew about Johnson, and nobody would have expected Moore to tell everything he had found out about Byron's raffish sex life; but the asterisks with which he sprinkled the letters he quoted as frequently denote bowdlerised expressions, suppressed opinions, in a word, whitewash, as any deference to the laws of libel. Moore was no turncoat, no Southey –

> He had written Wesley's life: – here turning round
>   To Satan, 'Sir, I'm ready to write yours,
> In two octavo volumes, nicely bound,
>   With notes and preface, all that most allures
> The pious purchaser; and there's no ground
>   For fear, for I can choose my own reviewers:
> So let me have the proper documents
>   That I may add you to my other saints.'
>   ('The Vision of Judgment', 1822, stanza xcix)

– and he was plain and honest about Bryon's politics; but his work is tainted by the un-Byronic timidity of the age in which he wrote, and our sense of what is missing is the more vexing because we know that Moore, and suspect that his executor, Lord John Russell, destroyed many of the documents on which it rests.

Later biographies of the nineteenth century are far worse. I confess that I never realised how far the Victorians were ready to go until I read the life of Lord John Russell's widow by her daughter, Lady Mary Agatha Russell, and Desmond MacCarthy (1910). Seldom can family piety have gone so far. None of the dramas and anguishes which Bertrand Russell makes so fascinating in his various accounts of his family (he was Lady John's grandson) is allowed to emerge. The result, necessarily, is that Lady John, one of the most remarkable women of her time, never for an instant comes to life, even though her biographers conscientiously follow Boswell and Moore by intruding as much primary material as they can lay hands on and fillet. The *Life* of Lady John Russell exemplifies the process by which Boswell's brilliant art was congealed, in pious hands, into the dismal official two-volume biographies which Lytton Strachey made it his business to discredit.

He might have had equal fun with the *Dictionary of National Biography*, the greatest monument to the Victorian way with worthies and unworthies. Perhaps Strachey was held back by respect for the memory of Virginia Woolf's father, Leslie Stephen, who was the work's chief editor. Perhaps he simply did not think of it. If so, it is a pity, for the *DNB* offered a wonderful target for his irony, beginning with the fact that the longest article in it is Sidney Lee's 110 pages (220 columns) on Queen Victoria. But then Strachey was in love with Victoria himself, and might not have seen the joke. Knowing Bertrand Russell so well, he would certainly have spotted the omissions in the article on Lord John: for example, the insanity of his younger son was not mentioned. And if someone had tipped him off he might have commented on the fact that his friends the Stephens had abused their position to write about the leaders of the abolitionist movement in such a way as to exalt the Clapham Sect, covering up its little mistakes, such as the dismal record of Zachary Macaulay as the Governor of Sierra Leone, and minimise the achievements of the Clarkson family. It is tempting to comment today, but to do so would be a digression. I can at least express the wish that somebody would go through the recent supplements of the *DNB* to see whether they really serve the gods of biography, or whether, instead, they simply reflect the pieties of our own age, as the original compilation did those of the Victorians.

Even in the nineteenth century not all was dark. Mrs Gaskell's *Life of Charlotte Brontë* (1857) brought threats of a lawsuit; Froude's *Carlyle* (4 volumes, 1882–4) scandalised the world. These were accurate indications that the authors had taken some risks in their desire to tell the truth. The joyful overthrow of Victorianism (which is all most people mean by modernism in this field) ensured that the twentieth century would be rich in good biographies as well as flooded by bad ones. But in the same age which saw such triumphs as Sir Rupert Hart-Davis's *Hugh Walpole* (1952) and Sylvia Townsend Warner's *T. H. White* (1967), the dismal process of suppression, hypocrisy and destruction still went on. Biographers might once again aim at being true Boswells, but the problems they came up against were still those which had impeded Thomas Moore: anxious friends, refractory widows, general nervousness and humbug. Even Sir Rupert could not be entirely explicit about his subject's love life, and even Sylvia Townsend Warner had to resort at one point to initials and had, at another, to suppress a girl's name.

There are other dangers of which we should be more aware than we are. To be personal for a moment: in the winter of 1984, having recently published a biography myself (of Arthur Ransome) I was interested to learn that the radio programme 'Critics' Forum' was going to discuss the year's biographies. I did not expect my own work to be singled out as the best that had appeared, though I would not have minded the flattery if it had been; I was not especially downcast that it was not deemed even worthy of a mention. But my hackles did rise when I noticed that all the biographies discussed, without exception, were those of literary persons – T. S. Eliot, Ivy Compton-Burnett, and so on. This struck me as both preposterous and significant. It was not something for which we could fairly blame Boswell, though his great work was devoted to an author. Nobody can suppose that if he had instead written the life of Pasquale Paoli, as he thought of doing, all our biographies would deal with nationalist generals. No, the reason must be two-fold. First, professional writers have an advantage over everyone else in the matter of leaving interesting papers. Second, writers are naturally more interested in other writers than in tinkers, tailors, soldiers or sailors. They do not always give in to this inclination, or we would not have such first rate works as Lord David Cecil's *Melbourne* (1954) or T. Harry Williams's *Huey Long* (1970). Whatever the reason, it remains deplorable, and unfortunately representative, that the lives of men and women of action were automatically ignored by a select group of connoisseurs. It was perhaps an accident that 'The Critics' did not discuss any lives of painters and musicians. It was no accident at all that they did not discuss a single biography of a politician, businessman, or philanthropist. And as to the record of lack-lustre lives, this seems to be something the literary mind is content to leave to social historians, as if it was of no interest outside that speciality.

It is possible to make too much of one incident, and even if I am right in thinking that 'The Critics' laid bare a common and deplorable assumption, it cannot be said that the fault is entirely theirs. When professional historians tackle biography they all too often write in leaden prose, solely to impress their colleagues. This curious prejudice, which has so little reflection in our daily lives – everybody nowadays likes to relax with a good biography, and nobody, not even historians, willingly seeks out the boring ones – reflects an impoverished literature and an impoverished history. It also makes life difficult for the biographer. In my *Life* of Arthur Ransome I tried to straddle the gulf, as my subject, very reluctantly, did himself. My reward was that some people liked the book in spite of the literature; rather more, in spite of the politics. I am pleased that they liked it at all; but I wanted readers to be interested in the common thread.

I complain of the stupidity of critics, which makes me all the more delighted that I do not have to complain of the cleverness of authors. As I have suggested, there is a lumpish, empirical quality about biography which keeps brilliance firmly under control. Norman Hampson has written a biography of Robespierre in dialogue form (1974). Hilary Spurling has successfully written a life of Ivy Compton-Burnett (1974–84) largely out of the evidence extracted from her exceedingly elliptical novels. No doubt writers will push the boundaries of the form a little further out in every generation. But they will not be able to reinterpret their business out of all recognition. They cannot emulate the evasiveness of Henry James, or the ingenuities of deconstructing critics. However they begin, they always in the end have to admit frankly that Napoleon died on St Helena and that Beethoven was deaf. If they were to leave out too much plain information their readers would dismiss them as cranks; indeed, I once read a biography of George Rapp, the American religious leader, which dissolved almost all fact in a mist of rhapsody, and was consequently no good to anyone. Biography is a wonderful discipline for writers. A biographer is less free than a poet, a novelist, a dramatist or a script-writer; less free even than a journalist. If he is wise, he rejoices in his chains – or she does. (It is a striking fact that many of the best recent biographies have been written by women).

Some of the biographer's chains are of his own contriving. Unless he feels a strong commitment to the truth of his subject, he ought not to touch it. If he does feel that commitment his conscience will allow him no rest until the job is done as well as he can manage (and even after publication he will be tormented as he discovers, too late, more mistakes). Other manacles are always being proffered by our times. In the West the biggest threat to a biographer's integrity is probably the enormous appetite for prurience and scandal. Elsewhere the censors reign. Free biography is an art practised in very few countries today. I may even claim that it is practised at its best only in English-speaking countries, for it is in them alone that a strong cultural tradition is coupled with a history of freedom uninterrupted by invasion or revolution: individualism has flour-ished. (As a scanty piece of supporting evidence I offer the thought that André Maurois was a most anglicised Frenchman.) In very few countries could Isaac Deutscher have written his life of Trotsky, and it is worth remembering that Trotsky was murdered while working on a life of Stalin. This lucky freedom is also a great responsibility. We owe others, as well as ourselves, a duty to preserve it. That means constantly trying to correct the continuing bias of our culture in favour of bowdlerisation and suppression (which co-exists with a taste for vicious tittle-tattle). People need constantly to be persuaded that biographers, and their readers, and above all truth itself, have rights. The point is far from generally understood. It is not so long since Russell Brandon had to print his biography of President Harding with long black lines in the places where extracts from Harding's love letters should have been. Some years ago an attempt was made by the daughter of Henry Clay Frick, the Pennsylvania robber baron, to win a legal verdict against a life of her father. She claimed, in effect, that it was possible to libel the dead, and that damages and suppression (not to mention heavy legal costs) were proper punishments for such an offence. Fortunately the American courts (warmly encouraged by the American Historical Association) reaffirmed the ancient doctrine that the dead have no rights in this matter. Living authors and readers do.

Danger will not necessarily come only from conservatives. The tide of modern salacity has not left the art of biography unsullied; new philistines may strike anywhere, in the name of vegetarianism or feminism or anti-racism, as much as in the name of family piety, patriotism or Communism. The important point is to fight back.

Biography at its best is a profoundly civilising force. It rebukes historians, with their bias in favour of generalisations, social forces, political machinery and machinations. It rebukes bigots, who forget the price in individual human suffering that their rigidities exact. It rebukes philistines of all sorts, by showing the richness in variety of human life and experience. It can display greatness, in a Tolstoy or a Florence Nightingale, but it also shows the cost of greatness to the ordinary people surrounding the hero or heroine. It can and should display their point of view, and set out their claim to respect. To be successful it must exemplify a due sense of proportion. It may satisfy the natural human taste for gossip, but must do so without malice or triviality (though every biographer should have a malicious streak, if only to ward off sentimentality). It can move us, amuse us, instruct us, and all in such a way that our sense of human solidarity is enhanced – it can even do this through the life of a monster, as Alan Bullock showed us in his book on Hitler (1952). It is an art to be cherished and an art which needs to cherish its warm relationship with common readers. Biographies written only for the *cognoscenti* cannot accomplish very much in the way of civilising society. And if good biographers ever lose touch with the common reader the gap thus opened will be filled with trash. Of that there is quite enough in the world already.

9

Neither Morbid nor Ordinary
Hilary Spurling

I should like to start from Sheridan Morley's definition of literary biography, in a recent Folio Society debate on the subject, as the 'Meals-on-Wheels service of the book world'. It is an epigram as neat as it is exact. It conjures up a pleasant picture of distinguished elderly people up and down the country seated by their firesides, musing in wheelchairs, propped up on pillows, waiting for their interviewers to arrive bringing news and questions about a past with which they may by now have little or no other outside contact. Reactions naturally vary (as they do, I believe, with clients for any other sort of Meals-on-Wheels) from eager anticipation through resignation and reluctance to outright hostility. When I began work on my life of Ivy Compton-Burnett, my request for an interview was refused out of hand only twice; and in each case I was sent for, long afterwards, out of the blue by the witness in question, on the grounds that posterity had a right to hear his or her side of the story. By far the more formidable of the two was the late Dame Joan Evans, who had written firmly in response to my tentative first (and only) approach, that she disliked Miss Compton-Burnett too much to wish to contribute to her biography. Four years later, after the publication of my first volume, Dame Joan summoned me towards the end of her life on a snowy day to her cold house in Gloucestershire where she received me alone, swathed in rugs, with the words: 'Let me tell you why I detested Miss Compton-Burnett...'.

For her, I was the receptacle into which she had finally decided to pour truths she had felt unable even to broach in her autobiography (Ivy had read this book when it came out in 1964, and pronounced it too discreet: 'It is no good to write about things, and then *not* write about them.'). Telling the truth (and in my experience it is often a matter of active exposure – tracking it down and ferreting it out –

113

rather than passive recording) is, of course, the prime purpose of biography. Truthfulness in this sense can become a passion. It is what drives relays of biographers all over the country to sit at the feet of distinguished elderly informants. It explains the endless hours spent in libraries, whole days hunting down a single marginal reference, weeks on end given to shadowing your subject up a blind alley, the months, perhaps years, spent posted – metaphorically speaking – outside his or her house on the alert for the faintest sign of movement within. It accounts for the biographer's daily routine – quite as monotonous as any private detective's – of asking questions, collecting facts, sorting, sifting, decoding, checking: poking and prying, in short, along lines laid down in Ivy Compton-Burnett's definition of gossip – 'just simple candid probing of our friends' business'.

This view of the humble, plodding, patient, persistent investigator – another harmless drudge, like the lexicographer – is a reality most biographers will recognise. It is at the opposite extreme from the sensational popular view of biographers as literary scavengers, jackals or carrion crows, disgorging what had much better be hidden, dismembering their subjects, sucking them dry, gathering in droves round their death-beds, flaying them sometimes even while still alive. This was the view ably advanced at the Folio Society debate by Germaine Greer, herself a biographer's victim in her own lifetime; and here I must confess that, when Ivy Compton-Burnett died and somebody told me that her publisher was looking for a biographer, I suggested myself with what may well seem indecent haste considering that she had been dead for less than a year. Ivy seemed to me then, and still does, a writer far ahead of her time – one of the great innovative novelists of this century whose importance has scarcely yet been recognised – as well as one of the funniest writers I have ever read. More to the point perhaps, she is a writer calculated above all to encourage inquisitiveness in her readers: 'We want to know the whole thing', as one of her characters says in *Daughters and Sons* (1937): 'Our curiosity is neither morbid nor ordinary. It is the kind known as devouring.'

My suggestion to her publisher was politely turned down, months passed and I thought no more about it until one day I had a phone call asking if I were still interested. I was so delighted I promptly resigned from my job. What Ivy's publisher didn't tell me was that she had commissioned someone else at the same time to write the same book without either of us knowing. Both of us eagerly accepted, and we both set to work. We didn't discover the fix we were in for six months, or it may have been a year, by which time it was too late to do much about it. The worst part of it was that, though we had never met, we lived opposite one another in London. By this stage we were of course dealing with Ivy's friends, many of them personally trained by Ivy in the arts of investigation and gossip, all of them taking full advantage of our situation. Perhaps they tumbled to it sooner than we did. At all events, they used to come to lunch with me, then cross the road to take tea with Ivy's other biographer. Or tea with her and drinks with me. Then they would go home and ring each other up, comparing notes. Documents were suppressed, divulged to one of us but not the other, used as a bargaining counter in return for the favour of an interview with a witness previously knobbled.

Events began to take on what you might call a decidedly Compton-Burnett twist. In fact – something I realised only much later – they ran quite closely parallel to the plot of Ivy's first novel (not counting *Dolores*, a much earlier piece of juvenilia which she disowned). This was *Pastors and Masters*, published in 1925 and set in a contemporary university very like Cambridge: what we should now call a campus novel. It deals with academics, their jealousies, competitiveness, cynicism and their perennial desire – running strongly to this day in so many academic critics – to write fiction ('Real books coming out of our own heads! . . . And not just printed unkindess to other people's.'). Two of them have found producing novels of their own such uphill work that, although one is already in his seventies, neither has actually done it. Suddenly, and almost simultaneously, each announce that he has at last got a novel ready for publication. Congratulations tinged with amazement and envy flow in from their friends until it gradually becomes clear that they have both written the same book or, strictly speaking, that neither has written a book at all. What has happened is that a mutual friend – another academic, this time a practising novelist – has died with his last book virtually finished. No one has read it. Each of his colleagues has had the bright idea of pinching the manuscript and passing it off as his own and, as other people slowly become suspicious, the two authors find themselves in an impossible position.

No more embarrassing, of course, than mine when I finally realised that I, too, was writing the same book as somebody else without knowing it. It was not simply that some of Ivy's friends had been stringing me along, nor even that she herself had anticipated and keenly appreciated precisely this sort of predicament. What I am trying to say is that, in writing a life, nothing is straightforward, especially not – in the case of literary biography – the extremely complicated, interesting and delicate balance between fact and fiction. Any biography must be in the first place an accurate historical record, a curriculum vitae as detailed, comprehensive, fully documented and scientifically correct as the investigator can possibly make it. The laborious assembly of facts may well take years. But, in order to convey this factual material, the biographer will generally, and I think inevitably, be forced to stoop to fiction. This is something often forgotten or discounted, especially perhaps by people who have not actually written a biography. Any reconstruction which is not to be purely external, and therefore superficial, must be quite largely made up. What you are doing, after all, is creating a character. Here the novelist is, and always must be, superior: the novelist has the edge because, as Anthony Powell has pointed out, he knows all there is to know about *his* characters. The biographer is stuck with such facts as he has managed to scrape together: generally a job lot, much too full in places, hardly there at all in others, nearly always with pitiful gaps and crucial explanations missing. At the same time, the biographer is forbidden to invent so much as a line of dialogue, or put a single thought into his character's head. Everything must be attributed, annotated, pinned down. You have to follow a set of rules quite as constricting and in their own way as inflexible as the legal rules of evidence.

A simple example of what I mean is Ivy's visit to Cambridge in May Week, 1911, to call on her younger brother in his rooms looking over the quad to the chapel at King's College. Ivy was in her twenties. She lived at Hove with her widowed mother and four sisters, all cooped up together at home year in, year out, seeing no one and going nowhere, with no friends of her own, no prospect of escape and no occupation save that of governess to the younger girls whose dislike she cordially returned. A photograph taken a few years earlier shows her dressed entirely in black: the family had worn mourning almost continously sincy Ivy was seventeen, and would return to it again in the autumn of 1911 when their mother died. To her sisters Ivy seemed – as she commonly did to outsiders in later life – harsh, severe, unapproachable, generally silent but cruelly cutting when she cared to be. What had this Cambridge visit meant to her? I knew she had been there from a chance reference in an otherwise uncommunicative letter and, although she herself never mentioned it, I guessed, from the way she wrote about it in *Pastors and Masters*, that Cambridge had made a crucial impact on her imaginative development as a writer. Eventually I found a witness who had seen her there in 1911: this was the late Right Hon. Philip Noel-Baker, a slightly younger contemporary who had greatly admired Noel Compton-Burnett at King's and who, sixty years later, vividly remembered the impression Ivy made: 'She knocked the college sideways. She was stunning. Absolutely beautiful, and she dressed rather to show it.'

How to reconcile the stunner who knocked Philip Noel-Baker sideways with the forbidding creature familiar in those years to her sisters? Or, for that matter, with the tormented, self-punishing, deeply repressed and clearly autobiographical heroine of her newly-published novel, *Dolores*? Sharply conflicting evidence had been a problem with this particular biography from the start. When I first began asking questions within a few years of Ivy's death, I was so much in awe of her austere public image that I found it at first hard to credit the tender, affectionate, often comical private Ivy her close friends described. I was quite unprepared to find how dearly many of them had loved her, and how deeply she was still missed. Others, admittedly, had found her literally petrifying (there are various versions of the story about the young man who passed out from fright at her dinner table, waking hours later with his head on his plate in an empty dining room from which his hostess had long since retired to bed). Still others, at a much earlier stage in her career, had dismissed her as a dull, dim, dowdy nonentity who scarcely spoke and to whom nobody dreamed of paying attention. She had undoubtedly been a tyrant to her sisters. To Joan Evans she was a menace: jealous, cold-hearted, unscrupulous ('Poison Ivy' was Dame Joan's phrase for her). 'I was a child of passion', Ivy herself once said to a friend, describing her tantrum at being given a pinafore when she had wanted a ball; and I certainly came to see her as passionate – passionately loving, passionately destructive – a person so helplessly prey to emotion that she spent much of her life erecting barriers against it.

This was a side of Ivy never shown to her sisters, who were the only people I met who had actually lived with her. They, too, had turned me down to start with, saying there was nothing they could tell me as they had scarcely seen Ivy in later life, had not shared a roof with her for more than half a century, had never in any case been close to her and could remember almost nothing about their early life together at home. This was a blow, considering the importance Ivy attached to family life in her novels. 'A family is itself. And of course it has things hidden in it. They could hardly be exposed', says a character in *The Mighty and Their Fall* (1961), whose own home life in some ways closely resembles Ivy's own. Dr Compton-Burnett married twice, presenting his second wife with five stepchildren, all under eight, and going on to father six more of whom the eldest was Ivy. By 1918 the sole survivors of this second family were Ivy and her sisters Vera and Juliet (the eldest boy had died suddenly of pneumonia, Noel was killed on the Somme, the two youngest girls committed suicide, while the five half-brothers and -sisters either left the country or made themselves scarce). All three had survived by firmly closing the door on their past. In my first conversation with Ivy's sisters, it was as though they reopened this door and went through it into another world, a world they had put behind them and now revisited for the first time in more than fifty years, exploring it apparently with as much curiosity as I felt.

My initial shock, when I reached their house, was to find that Miss Vera and Miss Juliet Compton-Burnett lapsed from time to time into talking like characters in their sister's books. I had brought two pot plants, one of which was unwrapped, watered, made much of in the place of honour while the other stood forgotten on the sideboard – 'like the stepchild', said Miss Vera when she saw it. She described the cloud that had settled on the Compton-Burnett household when their defiant eldest half-sister, who detested her stepmother, cut off her hair at Christmas, 1901: 'It darkened the day.' I should have been prepared for this: the pianist Myra Hess, who shared a house in St John's Wood with Vera and Juliet Compton-Burnett in the 1920s, described a similar shock in reverse, when she read one of Ivy's novels and recognised familiar Compton-Burnett turns of mind and phrase. Not that the characters talk like that in *Dolores*, which was actually written in the family home and published in 1911. For more than a decade after that, Ivy wrote nothing. With *Pastors and Masters* in 1925 she found a distinctive voice; with *Brothers and Sisters* four years later she began to draw on her own early life; and from then on she quarried her past as exhaustively as, say, Proust or Dorothy Richardson, digging it out to make building blocks from which she constructed her fiction.

In fact, she discussed it with no one. Like her sisters, she had

turned her back on the past by end of the First World War, and
virtually never spoke about it again. When her sisters opened their
door for me, it was like entering the world of Ivy's books – books
they had never read – from another direction. I framed my questions
from things I had seen or sensed in Ivy's novels; their answers
reflected the same things in a different mirror. I think they were as
astonished as I was at what they saw there. Time and again, if
anyone shrank from going further or looking closer, it was me.
Some things in their family seemed too painful, too delicate, too
private to be exposed. But, if I was reluctant to probe, they never
were. Their nerve was stronger than mine, at any rate to start with,
but by the end – we met regularly once a month for a year and a half –
I think we all felt that truth had been pretty well exposed.

Whether or not the truth needs to be told, biographically
speaking, is another question, and perhaps one that can hardly be
said to arise in this particular case. 'I like to know the exact truth
about the smallest thing', says the governess in *Daughters and Sons*. I
called the second half of my biography *Secrets of a Woman's Heart*
from a passage in *Parents and Children* (1941) where two adolescent
pupils are pestering another governess with personal questions as
to why she never married, and whether or not she had ever been
asked:

'I don't see that spinsters have any less success', said Isabel.
'Well, they have no proof that they have been sought', said
Miss Mitford.
'Have you ever been sought?' said Venice . . .
'You must not probe the secrets of a woman's heart', said Miss
Mitford . . .

Since Ivy's shrewd, detached and alarmingly observant governesses are clearly in some sense self-portraits – outsiders set apart
from the family they keep, in each case, under close watch – I took
this passage, and others like it scattered through all the novels, as a
kind of dare. Ivy left no private papers, kept no diary, wrote
probably some of the most non-committal letters ever penned,
destroyed her correspondence and in any case confided in no one.
These were precautions that came naturally to someone as expert as
she was at asking what she called 'impertinent questions': 'People
say that if you don't ask, you get told more, but I have never found
that to be true. I have found one gets told nothing at all', she

explained to her fellow novelist, Elizabeth Taylor, in the course of an interesting gossip about T. S. Eliot's second marriage.

Biography, if it can be said to be an art at all, seems to me in the first place an art of formulating the right questions, and asking them energetically enough. *Darkness and Day* is a case in point. This was Ivy's twelfth novel, published in 1951, a lighthearted, even frivolous comedy along Oedipal lines, enlivened by two of the toughest small girls in fiction who are shown making short work of a hopelessly amateur governess. It was not me but a friend who read it and asked the right question: 'It's all about death really, isn't it?' she said, and I couldn't think what she meant (she was dying herself at the time, though I didn't know it then). I understood only years later, when I came to write about the death in 1951 of Ivy's beloved, lifelong companion, Margaret Jourdain. Ivy was devastated, so much so that several of her friends feared she might not survive: a state of prostration hard to reconcile with a great many appalled and appalling reports of her behaviour to the much older Margaret in the months when Margaret's health had been failing.

These were the months in which Ivy was writing *Darkness and Day*, and incorporating in it a series of conversations between two deeply attached friends, Gaunt Lovat and the octogenarian Sir Ransom Chace, anticipating the older man's forthcoming death. The two cover the ground pretty thoroughly, discussing everything from the disparity in their ages, Sir Ransom's failing powers and the slim chance of survival in an after-life neither believes in, to practical arrangements for the funeral and for reading the will ('You can imagine me sitting there, having my curiosity satisfied', says Gaunt to his friend's considerable irritation: 'I shall do no such thing. I shall imagine you weighed down by grief.'). When Sir Ransom dies in the last chapter, Gaunt's shock and sorrow are genuine. Ivy, who had been unable in fact to prevent herself punishing Margaret for her own misery and terror at the prospect of being abandoned, was simultaneously working on this subtle, comprehensive, dispassionate and finally moving exploration of mourning and loss in her fiction. Margaret almost certainly knew nothing about it. Ivy never allowed anyone to see her manuscripts; by the time galley proofs arrived, Margaret was probably too far gone to read them; and she died ten days before the book was published.

I don't say that knowing how and why it was written improves *Darkness and Day*, still less that this knowledge is necessary to the reader's understanding or enjoyment, although I do think it alters his or her view of the book. It also casts light on the strange way Ivy transmuted her life into her work (the time lag once essential to this process being by now wholly eroded). In this sense, biography might be said to be at least a useful tool to literary criticism but, if it is to work at all on however humble a level, it must also exist independently. And here the biographer, having collected, collated and cross-referenced his facts, is obliged to make them cohere, to impose or discern some sort of pattern. Human life, as Ivy complained, is too shapeless to go straight into a book. The shape her life eventually seemed to fall into for me, emotionally and imaginatively as well as practically speaking, was an hour-glass – two distinct parts drastically divided by the First World War. The key would be one that opened the door she had slammed in 1919, and explained why she had locked it.

I think myself that there must be an element of impersonation, of construction and performance, in almost any biography. Perhaps the closest analogy is with painting a portrait: if two painters sit down to paint the same person – Manet and Renoir, say, who actually did this on the same day in the same garden – it is clear that very different portraits will emerge. One may be sketchier, the background a blur, with the chief emphasis laid on a particular gesture or movement, on a striking colour contrast, on the actual placing of the figure in its interior or landscape. Another may be minutely detailed, immobile, reserved, with no background to speak of – I am thinking particularly of Goya's and Gainsborough's portraits of their friends – expressive not simply of the sitter's character but of the respect and affection felt for him by the painter. My own feelings for Ivy were strong, and grew stronger. She taught me by precept and practice – as her sisters had taught me by example – that a biographer must never shrink from poking and prying. What she would have made of the likeness I finally arrived at is another question that fortunately cannot arise. As I got to know her better, I imagined I could recognise familiar traits all over the place in her novels, not only in the astute, watchful governesses who represent their creator in her professional capacity as an observer, but also in what seemed to me to be much fuller portraits, appearing at intervals of roughly a decade, of herself as a child, the eleven-year-old Clemence Shelley in *Two Worlds Their Ways* (1949); as a young woman writing her first novel, France Ponsonby in *Daughters and Sons* (1937); and again near the end of her career as the grimly humorous, eighty-seven-year-old Selina Middleton in *The*

Mighty and Their Fall (1961). 'I am old', says Selina: 'I have seen and heard. I know that things are done. Temptation is too much for us. We are not always unwilling for it to be.' It became a curiously reassuring as well as disconcerting part of our long, intimate, absorbing, one-sided relationship to look up, as I struggled to make sense of her life and work, only to find Ivy peering more or less sardonically back at me from her own pages.

10

Vivat Alius Ergo Sum

Andrew Sinclair

The writing of biography is more than a discovery of another person. It is a matter of self-discovery. If the subject of the biography is not too alien or repugnant, the writer goes through a painful process of immersion in another's life, a baptism by research. It is a dunking, not a debunking by a Lytton Strachey, who chose his *Eminent Victorians* (1918) out of disdain rather than sympathy. The cautious approach to the subject is deluged by the available material until the biographer has read more of his quarry's letters and heard from more conflicting character witnesses than he has about himself. Then there is the following process of separation and definition, painful and discriminatory. He or she, the subject, is not I, the author. I do know myself better. I am not he or she. Even if I do understand another so well, I must not pardon, but explain and judge. As Randall Jarrell wrote:

> Forgive, forgive, forgive no one,
> Understand and blame.

That is the role of the biographer.

Sartre used to expatiate on the difference between I, the author, and I, the subject of a novel or biography. His hero in *La Nausée* (1938), Antoine Roquentin, was trying to write the biography of a certain Marquis of Rollebon. He did not know why he was doing it and he would not finish the book. He felt himself an alien, a member of another species, hating the evidence of humanity and history. Everything was gratuitous. His work was unnecessary. This early novel, however, did not stop Sartre himself from writing volumes of biography and autobiography in later life. Curiosity about himself and his judgements overcame his sense of disgust and futility. He seemed to relish a confusion between himself and his subject. Roquentin, not his ego, was dead.

For me, both literary and historical biography are a plunge, an identification and a divorce. I try to choose subjects with whom I have sympathy and whose society I have considered. The process begins by an inquiry, whether there are papers and what are the terms of access to them. Biographers may not always have the troubles detailed in *The Aspern Papers*, but they do have the problems of family or state censorship. Access to royal papers, for instance, at the admirable archives in Windsor Castle is restricted and publication of a book is subject to review of the final work; royal copyright follows the monarchy in extending its powers over centuries rather than decades. If and when I am given access on reasonable terms to papers and witnesses, then I plunge. First, I try to fill my own library shelves with everything written about my quarry and his background. Then I go to my favourite libraries, the London Library or the Widener at Harvard, where topics are still listed by subject and are put in the stacks by subject, and I am given entry to the stacks. There I read books by the yard and have the relevant pages copied. Then a rough filing system, then the preparation for the quest – and inquiry by place and time and survivor.

There have been admirable works of imaginative biography, in which the search for the truth by the biographer is almost as significant as the subject of the biography. The voyage in the Odyssey fascinates more than the historical accuracy of Ulysses, King of Ithaca: Boswell is more intriguing than Dr Johnson. Livingston Lowes's *The Road to Xanadu* (1927), A. J. A. Symons's *The Quest for Corvo* (1934) and Will Wyatt's *The Man Who Was B. Traven* (1980) illuminate the inquirer, who comes like Childe Harold to the dark tower, or knocks like the traveller on the moonlit door, asking, 'Is there anybody there?' It is essentially a journey to all the places and people who can answer the right questions. And it is an imaginative journey, on which the biographer can stand and stare, look and hear with the same eyes and ears as the person he seeks to describe.

For me, writing a biography of the American film director John Ford (published in 1983), the trip to his birthplace in Maine was necessary, not only to find his birth certificate because he even lied about his given names, but also to stand on the Portland Tower where I know he had often stood as a boy. I also knew that, paradoxically for a film director, he had had very poor vision. And so, standing on the tower and looking for a long time out to Casco Bay with the salt wind blurring my eyes, I was able to see as he did and to imagine what I could not see, because I knew the history of what was there during his childhood. The paragraphs I wrote about this vision from the tower were the most praised in the biography.

Far below in the bay he could see the battle cruisers of Teddy Roosevelt's Great White Fleet when they came with outcurving bows and belching funnels into the harbour. Later he was to tell Cornelius Vanderbilt Whitney that he had spent much of his boyhood on that old wooden tower, gazing out to sea, or else going down to the Portland docks to watch real blue-water sailors. So his passion began for ships and those who sailed in them. To him the era of naval power and ironclad dreadnoughts was a boyish vision from a high eyrie, a dream of battle in a roar of broadsides. He told himself that he would become an admiral and roam the high seas, not knowing that nearly fifty years later he would film from a helicopter the firing of the last broadside from one of the last American battleships, uselessly into Asia.

From the observatory he could feel almost surrounded by the sea with the cove behind him and Casco Bay ahead and only the brick-and-board tongue of Portland running toward the Western Promenade and the interior of the land. He was a lookout in his crow's nest, an Indian scout on a cliff watching the small and vain scurryings of the people beneath. Even the steam and sailing ships in the bay seemed tiny in the distance, the little works of men in the sweep of nature. The beer waggons below pulled by their drayhorses were toys from this height. The ocean and the mainland made human beings and their doings as insignificant as ants in the wilderness. The city itself seemed small in the space of the sea and the vanishing of the continent into the west . . .

The very vision of the boy was special. His eyesight was poor and he could merely see a blur without wearing thick spectacles. When he took them off, his view of the world was changed to blocks of colour or the distinctions between light and dark. Only the movement of people or animals or machines would make a whisk of reference in his hazy universe. But the act of putting his thick lenses over his eyes would change the boy's perceptions into the definitions of the everyday world. So he could choose either way of sight and direct his eyes from the bright mist of partial blindness into the sharp clarity of normal vision. He would make his disability a special focus on what he wished to see.

Although this recreation of a sight was particularly suitable for the childhood of a film director, all people must discern in the arts and describe what they see. Even politicians and generals are said to have vision. Another's point of view is a proper position for a biographer to take. This special vision is also the place where the confusion of the writer and the subject is most fruitful. There is only one I, only one pair of eyes. Without visiting the sites of the past, there can be little comprehension in the present. And the very act of visiting makes the biographer more aware of the differences between his background and that of his subject. He defines his quarry better by defining where he never was before.

I once wrote a novel, *The Facts in the Case of E. A. Poe* (1980), which contained a short biography of Poe. It purported to be written by a modern man who identified himself totally with Poe. His therapy was to visit all the places where Poe had been and to write a biography of Poe so as to separate himself from his *alter ego*. The act of visiting all the areas of Poe's life gave me personally as well as my hero/biographer an exact opportunity to compare ancient and modern sensibility as well as historical awareness. A black comedy, the novel itself mocked at psychiatric techniques as used in biography, but contained a valid method of writing both historical and literary biography by description of place and comparison of time.

The chief pleasure in the discovery of another life is access to a personal library and a collection of papers. In the case of Jack London (my biography of whom was published in 1978), the Huntington Library in Pasadena has not only the bulk of the London papers, but his annotated books and photograph albums. More than a year of research there gave me entry into the mind of the dead writer and reader so accurately that I could ask the correct question about his death, apparently a suicide from an overdose of drugs. Reading through London's marked medical textbooks, I found a preoccupation with venereal and skin diseases, both of which were treated at the time with arsenic, either directly or through Salvarsan I established that London had been treated by arsenic for yaws and believed in self-administered medication. I found out that he displayed all the evidence of arsenic poisoning before his death, nervous instability and damage to his bladder and liver. I discovered the mixture of drugs he used for his injections against stomach attacks, a pain-killer and a stimulating poison. At this moment, the heirs to the estate showed me the very hypodermic syringe and the

vials of drugs he was using regularly before his death. For I had
plunged myself so deep into his reading that I could ask the right
question. It was not, 'Did Jack London kill himself?' It was, 'Was he
well when he took his overdose?' The answer was, not well at all. He
had regularly been taking overdoses of drugs, which his strong
body could survive. In this case, his weakened frame could not
cope. He had no intention of suicide. He tried to cure himself to
excess.

Asking the right questions in order to sift one's material remains
the most difficult art of the biographer. A flood of facts, as the
Kennedy Memorial Library provides, can make the task of
organization beyond the powers of seven maids with seven mops
working for half a year. Only a helpful archivist can suggest one's
way through such a welter of material, or an intuition of direction. In
the case of my biography of Warren Gamaliel Harding (1971), a
friendly curator, a copying-machine and a dearth of papers
shortened the time of primary research and forced on me an
intriguing method of writing about the life of an undistinguished
President of the United States. He became the subject of a larger
inquiry. It was more interesting to use the rise and rise of the
obscure Harding to the White House as a test of American political
institutions. Why did a poor or small-town background grow
presidential timber? Why did so many Presidents come from Ohio?
Do political conventions vote for a candidate or inflict one on the
delegates from a smoke-filled room? Even the title of my biography
came from a question, what made a candidate become *The Available
Man*?

According to Hobbes, truth consisteth in the right ordering of
names in our affirmations. Biography also consists in the right
ordering of questions in our examinations. It is particularly true in
modern biography when conducting interviews with interested
witnesses. The phrasing of the queries may suggest the replies,
particularly if the events are old and memory imperfect. Time and
the repetition of stories also embellish recollections of the hallowed
dead, so that a natural tendency to believe the actual witnesses of
people and events may end, as in the case of the man who shot
Liberty Valance, in printing the legend, not the facts. The practice
of leaving taped inverviews for posterity to adjudicate has become
the vice of politicians and their associates, a method of justification
from beyond the grave. Tapes, as Richard Nixon discovered, cannot
be questioned, only deleted. The spoken word as evidence is often

little more truthful than hearsay without a proper frame of inquiry.

Autobiography, indeed, is notorious as a method of whitewash and blindfold. The memoirs of a Bismarck, for instance rival those of Gypsy Rose Lee in hiding more than they reveal. The proper study of mankind may be Man, but not Myself. Even the writer of a secret diary such as Pepys hoped for its posthumous discovery, or else he would have destroyed it before his death: he too wrote not only for himself, but for the eyes of others and possible publication. If there were no biographers, the writers of diaries and autobiographies would have to invent them. Or who would ask the right questions and set their records straight?

I stress the process of writing biography because I do not distinguish overmuch between the writing of political or literary or artistic biographies. These all depend on the materials available, the approach to those materials, the ordering of them, and the nature of the biographer and his time. A biography is, after all, never finished. It exists only to be rewritten. From lack of other documentation and competition, the lives recorded by Plutarch and Tacitus will always remain seminal and basic to Roman studies. But their judgements have been questioned by playwrights and historians, from William Shakespeare to Michael Grant. No biographer can escape from the sensibilities and values of his age. We are caught in the same process of time from which we seek to rescue our subjects. As we explain others to our contemporaries within their terms of reference, so we date ourselves in front of our sons and daughters. For when they become adults, they will demand biographies written in the terms they understand.

Criticism of novels and plays, pictures and statues, suffers the same discredit in time as accounts of political manoeuvres and battles. There is always a New Criticism, a Theatre of Revolt, a Futurist movement, an iconoclastic school, that demands different perceptions and standards from those who depict their fresh leaders for their present readers. The Whig and the Marxist views of the vanguard of parliament or the proletariat have been made obsolete by their antiquated vocabulary. Psychological biography and now semiotic studies are also doomed to the poppy of oblivion because of the quaintness of their prose. Style, simplicity of expression and balance survive the verdict of the generations: philosophic and psychological structures and their related jargon do not. Xenophon will always be read on the subject of Socrates when Bertrand Russell himself is forgotten. In the pantheon of biographers, from the bards and court poets recounting the exploits of ancient kings and their families through Bede and Ibn Khaldoun and Camões and Vasari and the other national chroniclers of dynasties and discoverers and poets, their language is their passport to posterity. It is the way they wrote, not the purpose of their writing that engages us still. The style is the message, the medium is our awareness of time past.

The question is whether a modern biography of permanent value can now be written. Are the works of Richard Holmes and Michael Holroyd mere milestones on the way to that ultimate biography of Shelley or Shaw? The very process of writing a modern biography almost pre-empts its just conclusion. The flood of papers or the restriction of access to them, the decades of necessary research and the financing of those years, the modernisation of library systems leading to labyrinthine ways of finding material, all have turned the biographer from Proteus to Sisyphus.

The computerised catalogue of the Library of Congress, for instance, has changed card-shufflers into key-punchers, trying to find papers with numbers, and often failing. The increasing storage of primary sources on microfiche or within data bases makes these records less available to those with few computer skills. The tidal wave of taped material and the trickle of letters – how few literary or political correspondences remain in the age of the telephone – has altered the basis for biographical selection and judgement. The storing of sources of research in word processors risks both their loss beyond recall and their total regurgitation.

Paradoxically, modern biographers are both drowned by their material and stranded without it. Too much is recorded by new techniques and floods out beyond the possibility of channelling. Hesse's observation applies to every biographer – 'If man's first quality is his remembering, his second is his forgetting.' From that confused heap of facts that Chesterfield said was history, the biographer must recall selectively and forget widely in order to pursue a line of thought or even a well-made paragraph. A morass of material engulfs the refining of it. Some modern biographies seem to be written by word processor, so dense and inchoate are their facts. For the reader it is slow death by computer water torture, the dripping on the brain of innumerable drops of detail.

Equally, the dearth of written material or its loss within inaccessible memory banks creates gaps in research or different ways of presenting biographies. A collage by interviews, such as Jean Stein's and George Plimpton's book on Edie Sedgwick (1982), is the most modern of biographies. The judgement of the character is left to the reader. The biographer's job is to collect the accounts of witnesses, edit them and present them. No more. It is rather like the Dadaists claiming to be sculptors when they exhibited an ordinary hatstand in a gallery. The selection of the *objet trouvé* was the work of the artist and made the work of art.

The final barrier to writing a lasting modern biography is the lack of a common language. Homer and Vergil presented their biographies of heroes within the accepted form of the epic poem. Since the printing of the King James's version of the Bible and an available classical education, English biographers have shared a common style and frame of reference for their works. The mutual recognition has largely gone. The various schools of biography quarrel over their terminology and their constructions. The question becomes that of Sartre's Roquentin, whether it is possible now to complete a biography at all.

The answer is yes, in one way or another. But just as nothing is further from achievement than potential, so nothing is further from the lasting biography than the one now called definitive. We lack common terms and real definitions. We can only do our best by intuition as well as research to explore the life of another and to present it well within the understanding of our own generation. Schlegel once called a historian a prophet looking backwards. A modern biographer is a prophet looking at his chosen subject and inescapable self.

11

The Telling Life: Some Thoughts on Literary Biography

Malcolm Bradbury

Whatever the reasons for his reversal of good intentions, his monstrous metamorphosis, his ill-timed, misleading revelations, of one thing I am certain. I should not care to be in his skin, and the devil knows I am not ecstatically happy in my own. And, when his passion of remembrance is spent, I have no doubt he will wish devoutly he could cast off his sins and needle-pricking skin, like a strip-teasing snake in fright, and change it for another unrecognisable one.

(Caitlin Thomas on John Malcolm Brinnin, Dylan's biographer)

I shall give you a full and free account of my life without concealment and you can write what you like about that. But you will also give a clear account of the time you offered me Mary Lou and of the time you offered Halliday Mary Lou and had the offer accepted. In fact the biography will be a duet, Rick. We'll show the world what we are – paper men, you can call us.

(William Golding, *The Paper Men*, 1984)

When several colleagues of mine at the University of East Anglia decided to hold the conference on modern biography that has led to the present book, I was very taken by the notion. For there is no doubt that, in the academic world in which I spend at least part of my being, the idea of biography – and especially literary biography, which is my concern here – is something of a challenge, even a provocation. Today literary study is not greatly to do with writers but with writing, not with authors but with texts, not with factual records but with conceptual theory. And in this it seems to differ very largely from what goes on in what we call the 'real' world. Here writers' lives are often found far more interesting than writers' works, literary biography is, as the publishers' lists make very clear, a staple of the market, and a revealing record of the genealogy, psychology, friendships and associations, scandalous behaviour and stylish deviance that is so frequently the stuff of biographical enterprise will frequently provoke far more interest and sell far more copies than any actual book by the writer in question.

And so, it sometimes seems, we live in two ages at once. One is the age of the Literary Life, a time when the record of the lives, quirks and oddities of writers seem to constitute one of our great areas of preoccupation and our most interesting forms of narrative. Thus some of our most talented and readable books now are strong accounts not so much of the works of writers (those are for students) but studies of their personalities and natures, their relationships and fortunes. This is particularly true of contemporary biographies, the lives of the still living or the recently dead, lives which the published pages of the authors themselves seem to have shrouded in an obscurity we are ready to penetrate, and into which we can probe not just through documentary record but through remaining friends and witnesses, and even on occasion through the co-operation of the biographee him or herself. In some fashion the modern literary personality fascinates us, and of this kind of book we have many excellent examples: Richard Ellmann on James Joyce, Humphrey Carpenter on W. H. Auden, Deirdre Bair on Samuel Beckett, Carlos Baker on Ernest Hemingway, Peter Ackroyd on T. S. Eliot, Douglas Day on Malcolm Lowry, James Atlas on Delmore Schwartz and so on. Beyond them lie the many fine modern biographies of the great writers of the past, who have been rewritten for us, thanks not just to new archival materials but to new views of personality, as figures for the present: I think of Leon Edel's Henry James, R. W. B. Lewis's Edith Wharton, Anne Thwaite's Edmund Gosse, Gordon S. Haight's George Eliot, Edgar Johnson's Dickens, Maynard Mack's Pope and so on. The lives keep coming, and they have played a large part in shaping our contemporary sense of literary history and our image of the nature of the human creator.

Literary biography, then, is one of the main ways in which our writers become known to us. And we have only to look round us to see that the genre thrives, that its skills are substantial, and that it has a commanding appeal for readers. The subjects continue to multiply, and often it seems that it no longer matters whether they are major or minor, and whether the lives are flamboyant and scandalous or of the most breathtakingly tedious respectability. All is a contribution to the fullness of the record, the texture of the history, the fascination of the creative. In the great archive of modern culture, a culture extraordinary in its accumulation of record, the continuing potential for such projects is vast. Our libraries and universities constantly enlarge on the stock, and the accumulating records beg for the recorders: seven tons of Upton Sinclair's papers in the Lilly Library at Indiana University, a foot-high pile of *Tender is the Night* drafts at Princeton, the endless paper mineshaft of the Humanities Research Center at Texas, and so on. For the right interpreter with the right references, grants are not hard to come by. The stockpile of biographical armament has been greatly increased by contemporary scepticism and psychoanalytical awareness, and the biographer's dignity not as a hagiographic slave but as a serious and considered interpreter of human nature has grown greatly. And so we find ourselves in an era of literary lives of strong resonance and great mass, works where no stone seems to be left unturned, no oral source unspoken to, no postcard wandering through the mails left unretrieved. Indeed there are studies so substantial they outweigh, in bulk and cost, the entire published work of the subject, lives of such total fullness that – as with Joseph Blotner's two-volume William Faulkner – it seems impossible to believe that one single individual could have been so meticulous as to be able to live a life capable of filling so many pages, and still manage to write great novels as well.

And yet at the same time we also live in another age, not the age of the celebration of the literary personality but the age of the Death of the Author. Concepts of genius and literary creativity have been persistently stripped from us, and we now have many advanced literary theorists who firmly propose the tactical elimination of the whole idea of a safe, securable, person-like source of writing, a creative individual who is the only true begetter and valid first cause of the literary text. In modern terms, these theories are seductive. They tell us that writers do not so much write as get written, that it is not authors who construct books but readers, and that the only true object of attention is text as language. They tell us that 'literature' is an imaginary institution, that our canonisation of particular authors derives from suspect fictions, that the writer can in fact tell us little, and his or her recorded life can tell us even less, about the nature of the work. What we therefore heed is not biography but anti-biography, and the French Deconstructionist philosopher Jacques Derrida has indeed lately offered us one, in the form of a work called *Signeponge/Signsponge* (trans., 1984), which is a study of or a deconstruction of the French writer Francis Ponge. Derrida simply studies the proper name called Ponge, pointing out that the name, which clearly contains the work 'sponge', is yet a further metaphor arising from the work which bears that name as its apparently authenticating signature. The identity 'Francis Ponge' is none the less clearly the attempt to construct a proper noun from the mechanisms of the poetry he has written, or rather has written him.

This, I take it, is a clear example of the Death of the Author, and a considerable challenge to the biographer, of whom one thing is certain: he or she is always in collusion with the heresy of the proper name. Yet it is one of the triumphs of modern thought to prove to us that none of us actually exist, or that our assumed existences may, as we say, be 'demystified' – one of those strange words which of course means exactly its opposite. No longer should we assume that literary art is composed by innocent authors who have been conventionally born, grown up in the normal way, undertaken to imprint words on pages, be published, and addressed equally innocent readers in a pleasant and friendly intimacy. Today, for the higher theorists, the literary text – if, provisionally, we can agree that there is such a thing as a 'literary' text – is a psycho-sexuo-linguistico-ideological event, containing within it an implied 'author' who seeks to construct a narrative contract with an implied 'reader'. Happily this reader is supported by a kind of minder called a Critic, who is not in quotes, and can demythologise the entire process. This attempt to qualify the author in the text is also part of a strong agreement that there is in life no self-sufficient authentic ego who can be said to have authored it; the Death of the Author is part of the Death of the Subject. It surely has to be admitted that none of this sounds very promising or encouraging for the biographical enterprise.

So this is how we live in two ages at once: the age of the author studied, pursued, celebrated and hyped; and the age of the author denied and eliminated, airbrushed from the world of writing with a theoretical efficiency that would be the envy of any totalitarian regime trying to remove its discredited past leaders from the record of history. The situation appears peculiar. For, seen from the common-sense point of view, there is no doubt that authors do exist, in quite considerable numbers. We may not seem to think much of them compared with our pop stars or our politicians, and they are not in general greatly rewarded with public honours by comparison, say, with civil servants. But they have a visibility, even a certain fame, and they are unquestionably there; we can see them, touch them if we are lucky, and have them put their own signatures to their books in the bookstores. They gesture to us from our TV screens, offering their punditry on warfare and diet and sexuality and occasionally even discussing their own work. They have lives and wives and lovers and mistresses, and from time to time they go to jail, or go to France, or win a famous prize or a state accolade. Some will engage us with major ethical or political issues, others will engage our desire for form or beauty. From all they say and do it seems evident that it was they, and not writing in general, that conceived and developed and produced their books, that the images and preoccupations derived in some fashion from their own experience, that the human figures they represent may even at times have something or other to do with their friends or their enemies. They can tell you, if you ask them how they write, with pen or secretary or word processor. They have friends who will report on them, and the documentation of their lives is to be found in church records, passport offices and police files.

None of this can be denied, but in the refracting mirror of modern culture it can all be questioned. So how does our double view of the author, there and not there, come about? One simple answer would be that this is the difference between the public view of authors and those of the academic and theoretical specialists. In the common-sense world writers have common-sense existences. Here the reader takes the name on the spine of the book as a sign of a real name, a true person – though of course a person real in a special way, capable of bearing genius, creativity, moral insight, the qualities of the magus or the celebrity. Like most real people visible in the public eye the name acquires around itself an image, an influence, an attraction; it becomes the stuff of news, scandal and gossip, of vicarious public involvement. And perhaps it is in this way – as a higher form of gossip, scandal and vicarious engagement in the dramatic lives of others – that biographies often find their public place: though we also know that good biographies do much more, illuminating our culture and the conditions, the formation and the underlying perils and excitements of our literary art.

Yet the fact remains that the image of biography remains that of a traditional and popular form, its history predating 'serious' literary study and going back to Johnson's *Lives of the Poets* (1779) and Boswell's *Life of Johnson* (2 volumes, 1791). Indeed to this day – and especially in Britain – many of the best exponents are not academics but free-lance writers; I think of Michael Holroyd, Peter Ackroyd, Hilary Spurling, Humphrey Carpenter, Victoria Glendinning, Ann Thwaite and many more. Their work maintains the highest standards of scholarship and the pleasures of strong and vivid narrative. It is not, however, usually invested with the more advanced critical argument, and often it stands as a kind of adversary to it. Meanwhile in the academy a strong suspicion of biography seems to prevail. The New Criticism of the 1940s and 1950s, fighting its battle with old-fashioned literary history, turned against the 'Intentional Fallacy' (the author's intent), putting its faith in the centrality of the literary *text*; as René Wellek and Austin Warren said in their famous and influential *Theory of Literature* (1949), biography might frequently aid literary history, and our sense of traditions and influences, but, 'Whatever the importance of biography in these respects . . ., it seems dangerous to ascribe to it any real critical importance. No biographical evidence can change or influence critical evaluation.' Much the same was said of psychological study of writers, writing, and its effects on audiences. But these were only modest dismissals: the main task of literary study might be criticism, but scholarship was a necessary support. Today more daring proposals are in order, and scepticism goes even deeper.

To understand this it is necessary to remember the nature of literary study as a modern academic institution, and the rising role in that of critical theory. With the post-war expansion in higher education and the vast enlargement of the academic critical salariat, we have seen a great professionalisation and institutionalisation of work in literature. Like any growing church it has produced an ever-more complex theology and the breaking up of the broad church into schismatic sects. Some years ago I edited a book, *Contemporary Criticism* (1970), which suggested that this infant field was growing in importance. In 1985 it was replaced by a new book *Criticism and Critical Theory*, where the new editor rightly pointed out that the fifteen-year gap between the volumes marks a period of the massive transformation and extension of literary criticism. The change is one of mood as well as method. My own book, it seemed, was conducted in the spirit of T. S. Eliot's view of criticism as 'the common pursuit of true judgment'. But in contemporary literary study, devoted as it is to semiotics and structuralism, latter-day Marxism and feminism, hermeneutics and hegemonies, there is little that is common, small hope of truth, and not much to be said for judgement.

In these circumstances biography seems cast in an ancient and primitive role. This was brought home to me three or so years ago when I was invited, as a writer and a critic, to a university in Northern Australia where in tropical conditions many contemporary theories had reached a state of exotic enrichment. The department I went to was severe, up-to-date, not even called a department, the phrase 'English literature' having itself long since been demystified. Many of the faculty had been imported from British and American universities of the late 1960s and the 1970s, and bore the imprint of that heady, urgent and transformative season. They knew their structuralism and their semiotics, their hegemonic paradigms and late Althusserian revisionisms. Their students (mostly fresh from the sheep-stations) read Lacan and Cixous, and wrote essays comparing early to late Foucault. Literary works were not much studied, since who could agree that 'literature' existed? Yet, wandering through the institution one day, I found – like some alternative government, waiting to take over if the prevailing regime was toppled – a major institute of literary biography. People who wrote authors' lives talked to people who wanted to know how to write authors' lives, and strange matters were discussed: how to assess evidence, construct structured narrative, and explore the psychology of creation. Biography was not dead in the academy; it was alive and well but living in a quite different corner of the building.

From this situation, several deductions may arise. One is that modern academic study is divided: between the scholars and the critics, between the canonisers and the decanonisers, between those who study the writer and those who study writing. And this is partly true, but only partly. For strange tentacular relations do exist between modern literary theory and modern literary biography, or at least some of it. There may be some estrangement, but there is also certainly some intimacy. For the truth is that biography itself has come under the shadows of the era of suspicion, and indeed has been moving in that direction ever since Lytton Strachey. There was a time when biography's task seemed reasonably clear, and its methods obvious. It lay somewhere between hagiography and truth; the biographer celebrated the achievement, in public life and general fame, of the literary individual, and was the guardian alike of decorum and of accuracy. Respect and discretion were desirable job qualifications in the biographer, just as they were, indeed, in the biographee. But the age of genius and exemplary lives is quite over. We no longer acknowledge, in that way, the virtuously successful individual, and indeed we are no longer sure what constitutes the sum or significance of an individual. Biography has clearly grown far more sceptical of its subjects, more daring and critical in its treatment of them, and less sure of what constitutes their character or the truth and purpose of their lives.

In this it bears a considerable relation to what has been happening in other forms of writing, including, of course, literary writing itself, where the concept of a character, the sense of the clear evolution of a life, or the authority of the reporter have themselves become questionable. And if we are less certain of what constitutes the sum of a self, we are certainly far less sure what constitutes authenticity in writing. Nor is it clear to us how its significances come there. For not only critics but writers too have insisted on the discrepancy between the writer and the text, between, as T. S. Eliot put it, the mind which suffers and the mind which creates. Nor are we convinced by the certainties of our own narrative. The historians question history-writing and are forced to look again at the primary principles by which they have been used to structure historical narration; so, by implication, have biographers. Novelists and historians have commonly shared a sense of the ambiguous line between a fact and a fiction; and this has passed to biographers. Poets have come to doubt the power to create by word, novelists have come to question the coherence of a plot, dramatists the value of a single interpretation of an event. And so has the biographer, who is, after all, just another writer, writing abut those who are testing the limit not only of their own but of all writing's powers.

Biography is inclined to structure and assertion. 'The life of Ivy Compton-Burnett falls into two parts, sharply divided by the first world war', begins Hilary Spurling's excellent life of that author. Indeed, the interpretation pays off, for one thing dividing her own book neatly into two volumes and for another managing an effective account of why Compton-Burnett's early life acquires a ritual character in her later writing. At the same time we are forced to ask, how and why does it fall, and who did the pushing? And we are likely to be gratified by the fact that for apparently mischievous reasons Compton-Burnett acquired not one but two biographers, working simultaneously, yet giving varied accounts of similar evidence, varied structures for her existence. Biographies are, after all, plots, shaping and structuring the idea of a life; and literary biographies are the plots of the lives of plotters, who are likely to leave some trace in the biography of their own professional sense of plot's strange ambiguities.

But how can the plots be best constructed? In some cases, it would seem, they should not be constructed at all; many modern writers have sought to refuse the official life (as Eliot and Auden did), not on the grounds of misspent youths or hidden secrets, but on the grounds that the life of the author is not what is relevant. Other writers have in various fashions made themselves infinitely elusive, by masks and personae, labyrinths of personal disguise or chosen obscurity; so it has been with B. Traven and Thomas Pynchon, J. D. Salinger and in another way Vladimir Nabokov. The quest for such authors has been a difficult one, and the obscurity has been as much willed against the biographer as against all other forms of personal publicity. Three are writers who refuse to present themselves as familiar and recognisable wholes, like Samuel Beckett, that great writer of the characterlessness of the modern character, who did allow a biography to exist, but with him not quite in it. The strange desire of the biographer for the biographee has not, in short, always been reciprocated.

Indeed there is a way in which the modern writer has sought persistently to elude and shake of the modern biographer. This has been an important theme in our fiction; a brilliant example is William Golding's novel *The Paper Men*, about the war between the writer seeking to hold on to his soul against the erosions of the pursuing biographer, in a love-hate relationship that goes to the mortal limit. For the fixed life is the tombstone of literature; and the message of literature is often the flexibility of literary personality and existence. Writers need their elusiveness, and now they counterfeit their existence; the novelist as forger and faker has been a haunting figure in our writing. In *The French Lieutenant's Woman* John Fowles presents himself in the text several times: as social historian, as modern literary philosopher, but also, and most tellingly, as the impresario impostor. In Robertson Davies's recent novel, *What's Bred in the Bone*, the commonplace biographer is superseded by the

Recording Angel of Biography *and* by the daimon Maimas, who is there to insert the compulsive struggles hidden in art into the record. If there is a modern Death of the Author, the living author has curiously conspired in it. So doing, he or she has disappeared far ahead of us down the labyrinth of writing, with all its refracted images. It would seem that there is only one way for the modern biographer to go, if the quest is to be full, responsive to art's and the modern artist's nature. That way, of course, is into the labyrinth, where biography's own construction becomes part of contemporary writerly anxiety.